TRAPPINGS OF THE
GREAT BASIN BUCKAROO

C. J. HADLEY

TRAPPINGS OF THE

University of Nevada Press Reno Las Vegas London

GREAT BASIN BUCKAROO

Publication of this book was made possible by grants from the Nevada 125th Anniversary Committee (administered by the Division of Historic Preservation and Archeology), the Nevada State Council on the Arts, and the Nevada Humanities Committee. Without their participation this book could not have been published in its present form.

This book was funded in part by a generous grant from the Nevada Humanities Committee, an affiliate of the National Endowment for the Humanities.

Library of Congress
Cataloging-in-Publication Data
Hadley, C. J.
Trappings of the Great Basin buckaroo /
Caroline J. Hadley.
p. cm.
ISBN 0-87417-223-3 (alk. paper)
1. Cowboys—Great Basin—Interviews.
2. Handicraft—Great Basin.   3. Great Basin—
Social life and customs.   I. Title.
F789.H33   1993
941—dc20   93-22217
                                                CIP

University of Nevada Press,
Reno, Nevada 89557 USA
Copyright © 1993 University of Nevada Press
Book and jacket design by Richard Hendel
Printed in the United States of America
9   8   7   6   5   4   3   2   1

FOR SULLIVAN, AND THE REST OF THE

GREAT BASIN BUCKAROOS

CONTENTS

MARTIN BLACK: NOT CHANGING A LICK, 179

Responsible for seven thousand bovines, this cowboy has become
more than handy with a horse, hair, hide, and rope.

GLOSSARY, 191

Explaining some common buckaroo terms.

CREDITS, 197

POEMS

ACKNOWLEDGMENTS

For the ones who helped.

This book is offered in simple appreciation and admiration to the craftspeople who shared with me their time and talents and to the poets whose work appears herein. It is also for the dozens of people who helped and encouraged me through the long days of photography and writing.

Many thanks must go to the people and groups who offered financial assistance, including the Nevada 125th Anniversary Commission, chaired by Frankie Sue Del Papa; the Reno Rodeo Foundation; Nevada State Council on the Arts, with Bill Fox, Blanton Owen, and Andrea Graham; and the Nevada Humanities Committee, led by Judith Winzeler. Special appreciation goes to Ron James, chief of the Nevada Division of Historic Preservation and Archeology, watchdog for the 125th Anniversary Commission's generous grant. James had to bludgeon me to finish the manuscript, and accepted the job as project researcher.

David Zornes, general manager of Elko's Red Lion Hotel and Casino, and Dan Bilbao, owner of the Stockmen's Hotel and Casino in Elko, also helped, as did the kind and knowledgeable folks at the Western Folklife Center in Elko, in particular Meg Glaser, Tara McCarty, and Hal Cannon. And my Reno Rodeo Foundation–sponsored traveling photo show, a teaser for this book, was blessed and shown in several places: in Elko at the Cowboy Poetry Gathering; in Winnemucca at Shooting the West, thanks to Linda Dufurrena and Sheri Allen; in Carson City at the Nevada State Legislature, thanks to John Crossley; in Reno at the Washoe County Library, thanks to Martha Gould and Martha Green; in Elko at the Northeastern Nevada Museum, thanks to Howard Hickson; the new Nevada State Library, thanks to Joan Kerschner; and the Nevada Historical Society, thanks to Peter Bandurraga and Jill Cordi.

The photo show was also displayed at the Clark County Library's Sunrise Branch in Las Vegas and at Mesquite, thanks to Denise Shapiro; and in the State Capitol, thanks to Terry Sullivan, chief of Nevada's Department of General Services.

But many more were involved.

It was no small feat for Jim Polkinghorn to lend me Doug Groves, half a dozen buckaroos, and several hundred cows to trail from Mountain City to the Owyhee Desert. It was remarkable for John Ascuaga and his cattle drivers to share with me great country and a bellowing herd of thirteen hundred. It was kind of the Glasers of Halleck, Nevada, to invite me on their cattle drives. It was more than generous of Tom, Rosita, and the rest of the Marvels for introducing me to good horses and the Great Basin cowboy way of life. It was a bonus to be encouraged by William W. Bliss of Glenbrook. It was ultimate generosity for my friend Dave Moore to help review the copy. And thanks to Sharkey, just because.

During the writing of this book I had various freelance writing and photography assignments around the world, and it was a surprise to me to see how much I felt drawn back to dally in towns like Elko, Nevada, and Jordan Valley, Oregon. The book is a gift from home, from the high desert, which, after all my wanderings and walk-abouts, is the place where I wish to remain. It is for the men and women who work on the range and understand its handicaps and attributes. It is for the creative and the blessed.

TRAPPINGS OF THE
GREAT BASIN BUCKAROO

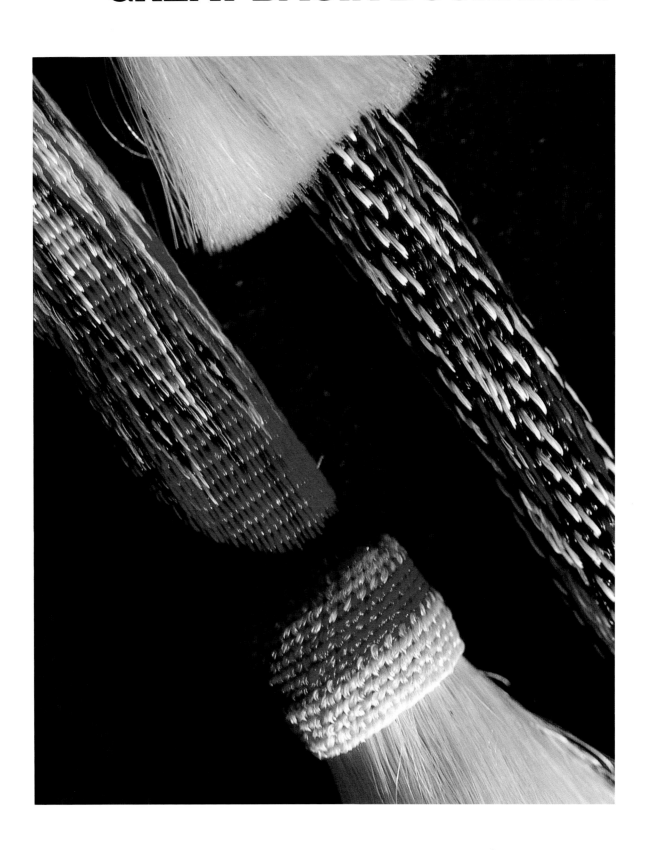

INTRODUCTION

Creativity comes from surviving alone in the outback.

Nothing has ever been as exhilarating or painful for me as the writing of these pages. Nothing from my youth, spent coughing in the English industrial city of Birmingham, could have offered me such a glimpse of a lifestyle so far from my own. Nothing from my education could have prepared me for the human treasures and talent to be found in the line shacks and saloons in the high desert outback.

In the beginning of the work I was fascinated, because I thought cowboys—with their tilted hats, wildrags, and tall, high-heeled boots—rode the range, chased cows, danced with straight backs and strong arms, and particularly enjoyed imbibing spirits, ogling women, and loitering in old, dusty saloons.

I discovered that cowboys are much more, and less, than John Wayne and his ilk suggested. The tenders of livestock work under tough conditions, as prescribed by Mother Nature, including drought, pestilence, flood, excessive heat, and numbing cold. They somehow survive on a corrugated carpet of brush and rock, their lives often hard and lonely, and yet they remain sensitive to their surroundings. They are sentimental, sometimes talking to themselves in rhyme, offering tender, funny, bared-soul verse that has led to many a sopping handkerchief.

I learned that the cowboy gear hanging in galleries, western stores, and museums was not done by long-dead Spanish craftsmen but by buckaroos who brought together practicality and beauty in their work.

I was inspired by humble independents who live the simple life they prefer, earning little, working a lot, and appreciating the sweet scent of sage after rain.

> Why do they ride for the money?
> Tell me why do they rope for short pay?
> They ain't getting nowhere
> And they're losing their share.
> Well, they all must be crazy out there.
> From "Night Rider's Lament"
> by Michael Burton

For more than a century, buckaroos have shared their love for the land, plus admiration for good horses and wild cattle. On long, cold evenings some cowboys would kill time by reciting poems about horses, women, the ranch—verse based on their own experiences or tales they'd heard from others.

Talented cowboys who weren't keen on words would create "trappings," useful gear for horse or rider. They would take the hide from a butchered cow, cut it into strips and braid it, making reins, reatas, bosals, hobbles, and quirts (see Glossary at end of book). Or they'd shave the manes off workhorses and twist the hair into handsome ropes, or pull the tail hair and use it to hitch fine horse jewelry. These complicated works of art are made from simple materials—cowhide, bone, horsehair, iron, and silver. The gear is useful and beautiful, often identifiable by the maker's style and talent.

Most of the stars in this book are Nevadans by birth or choice. They are people who appreciate the high desert and who share their home with the wild horse, mule deer, mountain lion, beaver, bighorn, and coyote. Nevada is typical Great Basin, an outback state with few people and fewer laws, home to some of the last big ranches of the West.

This book doesn't claim to be historically perfect. It doesn't claim to cover all the gear used by buckaroos. It doesn't even claim to be fair, in terms of craftspeople, in levels of talent, or items depicted. It simply is a celebration of the buckaroo's art. This book is offered humbly, and with great affection.

DOUG GROVES Out on the Range

Some western heroes believe they are blessed, and that God must

have been just another buckaroo.

During times spent alone at line shacks in the Great Basin, Doug Groves, working by kerosene lantern, braids rawhide into finely crafted horse gear.

Brush buckaroos remember every horse that ever bucked. They remember droughts and thunderstorms that scattered the herd, and the intense heat of a high desert summer. When winter's blizzards bring distress, lonesome cowboys living in the line shacks may dream about work in town, but when the sun returns, they never find reason to quit.

Cowboys have worked and lived on the ranges of the American West for over a hundred years. They have tended cattle, tamed wild horses, and spent months away from the comforts of instant heat and light. Sadly, their country and numbers are dwindling, their lives changing because of expanding urban population, pickup trucks, and a depressing switch from family to corporate ranch ownership. But for the lucky few, the cowboy world is much the same as it was before the turn of the century.

Doug Groves is cow boss of a northern Nevada cow outfit eighty miles from Elko. The ranch is larger than Rhode Island, covering over twelve hundred square miles of mesas, buttes, hayfields, creeks, and sagebrush. At thirty-one, Doug is responsible for almost fifteen thousand head of livestock, and with the help of half a dozen buckaroos he moves herds of cattle on and off the Great Basin deserts.

Doug and his cowboys work seven days a week, from before dawn to long after dark. Their pay—about $600 a month—includes food and board, which can mean good chuck and a warm bunkhouse or, just as easily, cold beans and a bedroll in the sage.

"This is a working cow outfit," Doug says. "We've got a lot of country to cover and lots of cattle, so we're just flat busy all the time."

Each spring the cowboys push pregnant cows, about a thousand or more at a time, away from the ranch. They move the buckaroo cook with the wagon to cow camp and set up headquarters on a sagebrush-covered flat. Huge troughs, with water trucked in by the irrigating crew, are placed around an enormous corral east of the camp. Smaller paddocks are used to separate the wrangled horses for the next day's ride. The troughs and numerous stacks of hay will sustain the herds as they move toward summer pasture.

When the buckaroo crew arrives, the cook always has a hot meal ready. He has prepared beef and biscuits, potatoes, gravy, and salad. There's pie, ice cream, Kool-Aid, milk, and thick, black coffee. A propane stove heats

the bunkhouse. An oil lamp lights the evening meal. Water is pumped from underground, close to the cowboys' teepees.

The horses are wrangled and saddled at four in the morning, a task immediately followed by breakfast of steak, eggs, potatoes, pancakes, and coffee. No lunch is offered on the trail so breakfast is huge, served just before the buckaroos get in the saddle to trot out to where they finished their work the previous day. They circle the herd until the cows start moving in the right direction, and then the riders gently coax the bellowing bovines into the brightening dawn.

Doug Groves has spent a decade working as a buckaroo on ranches in Nevada, Idaho, and Oregon. "For a while," he says, "I worked as a heavy equipment operator for an Elko County mine, earning $15 an hour. That was for ten-hour days and the money was good, but I preferred the buckaroo lifestyle."

Nick Whiterock rides point, to slow the runners and keep the cattle in a single bunch. Nick, a Paiute, has some cows of his own on the Owyhee reservation, but he shows up anytime Doug needs help. Nathan Kelly is also Paiute and the best roper on the crew. He and his wife and children live at the ranch,

Cow boss Doug Groves could make a better living in terms of money, but in terms of doing something that feels "just right," he chooses the buckaroo lifestyle.

Finely braided pencil bosals, these made from a black cowhide, are used with a two-rein outfit when a horse under training advances to the bridle.

and he works where he's needed, much like the cow boss. Two young punchers, Mike and Paul, work the flanks while Jon Griggs rides in the drag. Jon, twenty-five, handsome enough to be on a western poster, can ride, rope, play guitar, and sing.

"Cowboy etiquette," Jon tells a dusty greenhorn, "says that you never ride in front of another buckaroo." He laughs, then swings a loop and chases after a delinquent cow.

As they move slowly north, the sun comes up. Tiny wildflowers protected by brush offer a glimpse of yellow, orange, red, blue, and purple. An occasional holler rises with the temperature when cows get out of line, and by seven there's enough breeze to cause a fine dust to settle over the traveling mass of beef. The buckaroos can hear the birds and smell the sage, and they are somehow comforted by the sound of many thousand hooves shuffling down the trail.

"I'm a cowboy because I like it. I wouldn't want to do nothing else," says Doug. "You may be tied down doing chute work and be stuck in one spot for a while, but as a rule, when you're working with the wagon, when you're taking cattle out to the desert or gathering in the fall, you see the sun come up over something different every day.

"God must really like cowboys to give them that opportunity. He must have been a cowboy because he sure seems to favor them."

By noon black clouds are hovering, threatening rain. Doug looks around. Rain may grow grass, make the desert look and smell good, but it's depressing to ride in. He thinks of his young son Grant, daughter Katie, and wife Patti, who are back at the ranch.

During long, cold evenings at cow camp he spends time alone, slowly braiding rawhide into reins, ropes, and quirts. He likes the skins from old, skinny cows. "Really old, no teeth in their heads, the skinnier the better," he says. "You don't want any with fat on them. You want these red and white Hereford hides. You don't want black ones 'cause they leave dark pigment."

Doug's rawhide work has been displayed in museums and at cowboy poetry gatherings. His reins are used by cowboys all over the West. He fine-finishes rawhide bosals, makes hair tassels with rawhide buttons. He also twists and braids rawhide reatas, which turn into seventy feet of strong and flexible rope.

There are many ways to get hair off a hide. Some people use lime. Others soak it in hot water until the hair separates from the skin. The hide can be put in a super-cold creek that runs so fast the hair comes off. A hide can be scraped or the hair can be left to rot off, which takes about four days in warm weather, up to three weeks when it's cold.

When a hide is limed, it turns white and takes the real pigment out. If a hide is allowed to rot, it gets thick and tan-colored. Doug prefers scraping. "Scraping them is the hard work, but you get your prettiest color that way," Patti says. "Doug usually dries them out and then scrapes them, because he likes a lot of color in his rawhide."

Doug is as skilled a craftsman as he is a cowboy. Often when he starts using a set of reins, someone will buy it straight off his horse. Groves, who sells the gear to supplement his income, hasn't kept many pieces he's made.

He knows a lot of hair twisters—cowboys who make mecates, usually from horses' manes—but he wouldn't "roach" a horse for any of them. "Taking a mane off your horse is like selling your soul to the devil," he says. "That's bad

medicine." Then he laughs. "Of course, you could take hair from workhorses or horses that don't belong to you!"

When the buckaroos get back to camp they wrangle horses for the next day's drive. If they get in early enough, they ride colts, shoe horses, practice roping, or, if necessary, doctor sick animals. After an enormous supper, the cow camp grows quiet.

In a few weeks, when all the stock is on summer range, the cowboys will set up small camps with a teepee and makeshift corral to serve as locations for branding. The branding work goes on for weeks until the fattened steers are shipped to market in late summer. Soon after that, the cowboys return to the desert to bring the cattle back home to winter feed.

"For the fall drive, most of us go out in the beginning, to get the majority of the cattle started in the direction of the ranch," says Doug. "Then I'll leave just two guys out there to keep them coming. The rest of us will be back at headquarters, catching them as they come in, working them, separating them into classes—pregnant cows, slick [unbranded] calves, bulls, and heifers. We'll take out the cull [inferior] cows and the dry cows to sell with the

opposite:
When Groves cuts and prepares strings, he works on several pieces at a time. The thinner strings are reins (with two eight-strand and one twelve-strand shown). The thicker strings are for a twelve-strand romal and two sixteen-strand hackamores. These pieces are in the early stages; buttons and other finishing touches will be added later.

Six-strand twisted rawhide reata showing rolled hondo. The twisted rope is quicker to make but can't be spliced. If a braided rawhide rope breaks, it can be fixed.

rest of our steers." That work takes pretty much all fall. Then the cowboys wean the calves from their mothers in winter and work in the calving barns before the spring drive starts again.

"When you're young," explains cowboy poet and buckaroo Waddie Mitchell, "you're willing to live at places you wouldn't believe people inhabit. I was a buckaroo because it helped me to hang on to tradition, and it meant making a living on horseback." And Doug has a similar philosophy. Cowboys may dream about the romantic life they lead, but eventually they find the tradition has to flex a bit. Even though they still get up in the freezing cold at four in the morning, most of them will take advantage of pickup trucks, electricity, and hot, running water, when they can find them.

"I wouldn't have dreamed of getting off my horse for anything when I was young," Waddie says. "Now I fix machinery and muck out the barn."

The reality of today's ranch work is endless chores while working with tough horses and wild stock. Sometimes cowboys get hurt. They worry about the low price of beef, the high price of a vet, and the inflexibility of some government officials. They have no idea what they'll do when they're too old or bent up to ride. Many of them are alone because it's tough to find women who can tolerate their lifestyle. Even so, Doug Groves and his buckaroo friends will tell you their way of life is best, because they treasure their freedom.

"A lot of people think we're crazy doing what we do," Doug says, "but riding good horses, trailing good cattle, the land and good weather, that's better than a whole bunch of money."

He tugs at his handlebar mustache and adds, "So you get bucked off a time or two and it rains some. At times it snows to beat hell, and the frost can cause pain that's tough to express, but when the sun comes out and the flowers bloom, when the cattle are moving together, the loop catches two hind feet, and the branding iron burns even, then God smiles and everything is sure worth the trouble."

Rawhide reata. The best work shows even braids, uniform-diameter rope, and a perfect hondo.

After the cavvy is brought in, each buckaroo calls out his choice and the cow boss ropes his mount for the following day. Groves selects a bay horse, a tough one, to carry him around the twenty-five-mile outside circle.

THE BRANDIN' CORRAL

When the west was all onsettled and there wasn't no bob wire,
They had a way of workin' that was supthin' to admire.
Every thing was done on hoss back, and I've heard old timers talk
How the kids in cattle countries didn't hardly learn to walk.

They worked cattle in the open, and they laid 'em on the ground.
It was cuttin', flankin', ropin', and a tyin' critters down.
But the present cattle raiser ain't so strong fer that idee,
And he has a way of workin' that's as different as can be.

'Taint so hard on men and hosses, and it's better fer cow brutes
When you got a place to work 'em in corrals and brandin' chutes.
When we heard of brandin' fluid, fust we took it fer a joke.
Jest to think of brandin' cattle when you couldn't smell no smoke.

Well a feller cain't deny it that the new way is the best,
Fer there's been a heap of changes in the ranges of the west.
Most of outfits then was bigger, and a cow was jest a cow,
And they didn't stop to figger things as close as they do now.

Bruce Kiskaddon

FRANKIE DOUGAL Country Spinner

This feisty woman would rather make mecates and listen to frogs than take

a trip into town.

If a rope could tell a tale, this soft and fine one, made of human hair taken from members of Frankie's family, could write a novel. Frankie can twist a rope out of anything.

Frankie Dougal was raised in Idaho eighty miles from the nearest town. Her family ran horses on the Owyhee Desert and made a living selling mustangs for $5 a head. She still lives close to the place of her birth in an isolated canyon near South Mountain, but it is too far from a post office to give her an Idaho address. She gets mail through Jordan Valley, Oregon. The mail and groceries are delivered by stage those eighty miles, and her telephone is shared by thirteen other ranches.

Part of her ranch house has a sod roof, and a dirt-floor cellar keeps supplies cool summer and winter. When she's outside, she wears a stingy-brimmed hat and western clothes, and she's quick to offer visitors a bite to eat and a cheeky grin. She enjoys holding court in her enormous kitchen. It's big, twenty-four by fourteen feet, and she can serve fourteen at a sitting. "I couldn't live with a tiny kitchen," she says.

The willow and juniper corrals at the Dougal Ranch are common throughout the Great Basin, partly due to limited resources. Frankie displays her wares along with chinks made by daughter Charlotte and rawhide bosals made by husband Chuck.

As a mecate maker (pronounced McCardy), she feels lucky when she can get the special blue-gray mane hair that seems to come only from horses that run on the Owyhee Desert. "In Nebraska you don't get hair like that," she declares. Although she still rides with the best, she likes working with her hands, spinning—tight—an enormous variety of beautiful ropes.

Of four siblings—one boy and three girls—she's the only one who stuck to ranching. The Dougal Ranch used to be surrounded by sheep country, but when the government restricted the roving bands after the turn of the century, the family changed to cattle.

Frankie Drummond Whitby married Chuck Dougal, the youngest son of nine kids in a Boise family, in 1939. "When he was fifteen years old he came over here to Juniper Mountain. That's where I met him or he met me," Frankie says. "He was a city boy, but he didn't like the city. He just liked ranching, and that was it."

At seventy-three, Frankie remains funny and tough and smart. She says her mother, Clara Drummond Whitby, a pretty tough lady herself, learned to twist hair ropes from an old Mexican man named Jesús.

"My mum made ropes because she had to. She just done it because they needed ropes for lashes 'cause the family packed horses a lot." Clara's horse-hair mecates were beautiful. "I kept one of the last ropes Mum made before she died," Frankie says. "I just kept that one."

When Frankie was about nine, Clara taught her the art of mecate making. Until about twenty years ago, when a gravel road was built to get kids on the line to school, the only way to town was by horseback or by team and wagon. "My brother packed the mail here for twenty-four years, horseback, seventy-six miles round trip. He came down one day and went back the next." The road is bladed now, with snow cleared after every storm, and mail is delivered to the ranches twice a week.

"I've been around here all my life," she says with a smile. "The little lake in front is Dougal Reservoir, built in '57 because the original dam broke. The first one was built by an old fellow and a team back in 1915.

"My folks homesteaded eighty miles out of Jordan Valley, and my mother taught us not to be scared of anything. There were a lot of coyotes. One would be rabid and would stagger and slobber at the mouth and run into bushes. Momma said, 'Don't be scared of them,' and probably we had no shoes on, probably didn't know what a shoe was hardly, and we'd run to the house in our little bare feet. Luckily, there was never much snow down in that canyon."

When Frankie was about five years old, the family moved closer to Jordan Valley and homesteaded thirty-eight miles from town. Some of the older kids were boarded out in town. "We had to be more accessible because four of us little brats had to go to school, you know."

Frankie Dougal has made more than a thousand ropes and is never surprised to find one. She had a little book with styles and colors written down, "but it seems like I make it different every time." She often orders hair from a horse-killing plant in Nebraska. She used to get it out of Santa Rosa, California, but the plant burned down.

Hair is sold by the pound, often mixed and thrown in a box. But Frankie likes to get a lot of white, so last time she ordered fifty pounds of white, twenty-five pounds of sorrel and twenty-five pounds of black. "White's harder to get because there are less white horses," she explains.

If hair is bloody or dirty, she washes it in detergent and water and then dries it for several days. After combing it, she sorts the hairs by color, dropping them in a pile, a few hairs at a time in different directions. This is called "picking" the hair. She then rolls the hair in buns or rolls, with all the colors separate. After that, it's ready to spin.

Some mecate-makers prepare the hair with home-built picking machines, but Frankie likes to do it the hard way, by hand. "If it isn't picked just right, it doesn't spin well," she says. "You'll have knots and all kinds of problems." Most of Frankie's ropes are made from sixteen thin strands of hair twisted together, and the most popular finished rope is five-eighths of an inch in diameter. She can change the size of a rope by spinning more hair into each string for a thicker rope, less hair each string for a thinner rope. A rope's size depends on its use. Frankie's hackamores are made from extra-thick strings and used on young horses. Her fiadors (or Theadores) are the size of a pencil and tied around the horse's neck. She also makes hat bands and has made miniature sets of reins for show. Her daughters, Helen and Charlene, used to have long hair, and when they cut it, Frankie made a soft and beautiful human hair rope. Today she collects hair from her granddaughters.

Helen, who married a cowboy from Golconda, Nevada, is a hair twister, too. Charlene makes chaps, chinks, and leather gear using an electric sewing machine, powered by a generator, at the home ranch bunkhouse. Husband Chuck makes bits, spurs, and cinches from hair Frankie spins and he braids the buttons on the end of her ropes to finish them off.

"Making mecates takes a lot of practice," she says. "You have to feel it in your fingers." She usually works with mane hair. "Tail hair makes a wonderful rope, but it's coarser," she says, and can bother the horse. She is partial to thoroughbreds' hair "because it's softer."

Frankie and Chuck's ranch consists of over thirty-two hundred deeded acres, and their cattle forage on several thousand acres of federal land for four and a half months a year. Their son Ben's ranch is another twenty-five hundred acres. Together, they take care of the livestock—including calving, weaning, doctoring, and feeding in winter—with the help of Charlene and her husband, Frank Stanford, who live a couple of miles up the creek. They irrigate several hundred acres of wild hay using water from the reservoir.

Frankie picks chokecherries, wild currants, and gooseberries and cans

them in summertime while the others cut and bale hay. There is enough to feed their two hundred and fifty head of mother cows as well as calves, bulls, and a few horses over the long winters. The snow can come in October and often lasts through April.

"We have about six months of winter, and I love it. If it snows in here, I can just work with hair all winter," Frankie says. Sometimes winters are not so hard and they have hay left over. She grins. "That's just like money in the bank."

The cost of a Frankie Dougal rope is about $75, which is less than most people expect to pay for quality work. "A cowboy is the poorest paid man in the world, you know," says Frankie, who makes her ropes to order. "People phone me from everywhere and tell me what they want. Black with a little white in it, maybe a bit of sorrel, maybe run one sorrel string through it. Most of them aren't particular about the color, they just say five-eighths or three-quarters. Some want seventeen feet, otherwise it's twenty-two."

When the kids were growing up, Frankie bought a little house in Jordan Valley because the snow got too deep to commute to school. She knew her kids had to be educated even though she didn't like town. "I couldn't stand it," she says. "I went crazy. Trucks would go by all night long. The house didn't have a foundation, so Chuck and the hired man brought me down some baled hay and packed them around the bottom for insulation so that we could keep warm. I hate the dark, and one night I could hear this wild horse chomping around the house eating that hay."

She was scared in town, but the sounds at the ranch don't bother her. "You don't pay attention to crickets and frogs croaking at night, birds singing and coyotes howling—we love that."

Frankie Dougal has displayed her work at the best shows and museums in the country, including the Smithsonian Institution in Washington, D.C. She's often asked to appear, too. "Once, for the Trappings of the American West show in Flagstaff, Arizona, they invited me to be there, but my sheep were lambing, my kids were trying to calve out cows. I couldn't go 'cause I was kinda needed here on the ranch."

Frankie's horsehair cinches will last for twenty years. Her ropes will last a lifetime. As Frankie spins in winter, Chuck works on steel bits and spurs in his workshop. He rigged up a machine so Frankie can do most of the work alone. She can spin and turn the strands but has to have two people help her twist and finish the mecate.

Chuck Dougal watches his wife cook, clean, spin, twist, and entertain, almost at the same time. He sighs and says, "You sure gotta run a long way to catch Frankie."

Cattle heading out onto the Owyhee Desert at the start of green-up in the spring, an event known as "turn-out" to the cowboys.

OLD COWBOYS DON'T DIE

As I walked out in the streets of old Prescott,
I seen an old cowboy as sad as could be,
His neck was all dewlaps, his hide was old leather,
His joints was as stiff as a dead cedar tree.

One eye was as dim as a taller-dip candle,
T'other was hid by a patch black as sin.
He'd fought Father Time in one Hell of a battle,
An' he'd give it up that he just couldn't win.

Then here come some wimmen a-steppin' and prancin',
They give this old puncher the "come-hither" eye.
He jumped up and follered 'em just like a yearlin'.
You and me knows that old cowboys don't die.

Gail I. Gardner

SHORTY PRUNTY

Copper Mountain Cowboy

A lifetime working rawhide, a lifetime on the range.

Shorty Prunty is bigger than his name. He's tall and lean and has a broad smile and pale gray hair. His ranch is in an isolated area called Charleston in a broad valley that sits at the foot of Copper Mountain north of Elko, Nevada. Water for his stock comes from Copper Creek, which has never dried out, and Shorty's range runs for miles to the head of the Bruneau River. Winters are hard. Sometimes, when the snow is deep, he has to use a team of horses to feed his cattle or use a snowmobile to check the waters.

Shorty's life has revolved around cows and horses. He has ridden the range so much that he is a member of the exclusive 100,000 Mile Club, which means he's covered at least that many miles in the saddle. When he was just a little boy, his family ran "many, many horses." He had a rodeo string of bucking stock and worked as an arena pickup man.

For several years in the sixties, Shorty left the ranch and worked as a rodeo stock contractor. He took animals to Los Angeles to the National Rodeo Finals in 1964, taking third place for best bareback horse. "It come right off this ranch. Called her Broken Blossom. Good rodeo horses can perform in every condition. In a building, in bad weather. Oh, I loved them," he says. "Some of them were thoroughbred type horses, the best kind. Old spoiled saddle horses were the best rodeo stock."

He quit the sport in 1967 after he and his brother put on the National High School Rodeo Finals in Elko, "a big production." He says there were too many other things he'd rather do, like hunting, trapping beaver, working horses and cattle. For decades he has run a hundred horses—raised for pleasure and as hunters—into Idaho on and off the Diamond A Desert. Shorty still runs a roundup every fall when he returns the horses to the ranch for the winter. In spring he pushes them back to the desert.

Shorty Prunty's braided reatas are sometimes made of cowhide, which varies in color, sometimes of deer hide (the light one).

"You are usually awfully busy on a ranch," Shorty says. "In between, it's nice to get into something like rawhiding."

He owns a house in Elko but prefers living at the ranch and braiding buckskin. "I'm the only one in the country that's doing buckskin reins, I think. It's better than rawhide. One set of buckskin reins will outlast two or three sets of cowhide reins."

Hides are easy to get because Shorty runs a hunting camp each fall, and the hunters take the deer meat and leave the skins behind. He started the hunting camps around 1941. His clients hunt for mountain lion as well as deer. "Mountain lions are like a shark in the ocean. They are awfully hard to get because there's no pattern to them. A mountain lion likes horses and deer and can kill six hundred or seven hundred deer in his lifetime—one a week."

He enjoys making reins from the hides of cattle and wild game. He begins the process by cutting a long, narrow strip from each hide, starting at the outer edge and cutting closer and closer to the center. He can get a string more than two hundred feet long from a small deer—enough for two sets of reins.

In the barn he has a mechanized string cutter. It's primitive, but he thinks it's the best way to cut strips from a hide. "You can cut a thousand feet with this machine and there won't be any difference in the strings," he says. The contraption cost Shorty fifteen cents and consists of an old knife blade, two horseshoe nails, and a piece of wood for a seat. "When you pull hundreds of feet of string at a time," he says, "you want to be comfortable. This is called a splitter. If your string is just slightly damp, it works beautifully and splits that rawhide perfectly even."

Shorty puts eight to twelve strands in a set of reins. "For twelve strand you cut them thinner, but the finer they are the more apt they are to break." He dyes some strands with leather dye: "Anything to dress them up a little."

He was born on the ranch in Charleston shortly after his father bought the place from his uncle. "Grandfather Prunty lost three brothers in the Civil War. He was seventeen in 1861. He went to Texas and was on the Oregon Trail, but when he got to Wells, Nevada, he was broke. He went to chopping posts, for a nickel apiece, for fences." In about 1885 Grandfather Prunty homesteaded at Charleston.

Several of the Pruntys were rawhide braiders, including Shorty's father,

cousins, and brother. "There's about seven or eight different buttons my brother knew," Shorty says. "He could look at one, go home and start fooling around, and pretty quick he'd have it tied." Buttons hold the reins away from the horse's neck so sweat won't travel up the reins to the rider's hands. Over time, buttons have come to serve a more decorative function.

Shorty was braiding cowhide by the time he was twelve years old and turned to braiding buckskin around 1966. He takes hair off the skins by leaving them in a warm spring for a few days. The hair becomes loose and slips off the hide, leaving it smooth. In cold water the process works the same but takes two or three weeks. He cleans the hides by soaking them in a mixture of Ivory soap, neat's-foot oil, and water. "Let it soak, that's old Indian style. You leave

Shorty is a member of the 100,000 Mile Club, honored because he has ridden at least that far horseback. He sighs when he thinks of all the hides he has waiting in the barn, ready to be cut into strings for reins, bosals, and reatas.

As one of very few
cowboys who use
several shades and
colors in his braided
work, Shorty says,
"I think they're
pretty that way."

it until you can make a bubble and squeeze air through it." The Indians would
smoke it by hanging it over a sagebrush fire, but Shorty doesn't bother with
that step. After the hide has dried somewhat and is barely damp, and hard but
not tanned, Shorty puts it in moist sawdust so it will stay easy to work.

He doesn't use the neck of an animal, because it's too thick. He claims
a really good rawhider only uses the belly and the sides. He prefers big old
deer with thick skin, and, because he gets his skins from hunters, he has to be
careful of weak spots around the bullet holes.

He rough-cuts the strips a half inch, quarter inch, or three-eighths of an
inch wide on his home-built machine. He says it's easier to cut the hide when
it's stiff, easier to braid when it's wet. He does most of his braiding in March
after the strings have been stretched and dried on a fence. "The string's wet
when you cut it," he explains. "If it's freezing at night, there will be parts that

freeze and parts that will dry. In March you get those nice warm winds, and if you put a wet string on the fence, it will dry evenly." He adds, "Tanned hides make soft reins, but rawhide makes stiffer reins with nicer body."

In all it takes thirty hours to make a set of reins. He figures he spends fifteen to thirty minutes extra for each button. "My buckskin reins are $250 a set, and if I can't get that, then I'll leave them for the kids. It's real intensive work, putting those dumb knots on them. I haven't sold any yet!" But lack of sales doesn't matter much to this cowboy. He likes working the hide.

He puts tension on each new string he cuts, breaking it two or three times in order to discover the weak spots, so he knows the rest will be good and strong. If he makes a mistake when braiding, he pulls the string out and starts again. "I just cuss them when they come out wrong." When he needs to put in a new string he brings the old one out of the braid, tapers it to keep the work smooth, then buries it next to the core. The beginning of the new string is also tapered and buried.

He doesn't look at his braiding as an art. "It's something to do. You get into it and it's satisfying to make something nice that you can use and pass on to somebody. The best ones I do are the ones with fine strings. They're probably from a doe hide or a small buck. They're fine and feminine."

Some braiders use other kinds of hides. "If you are using cowhide, you need either a Guernsey or Jersey," Shorty says. "A Hereford or Angus isn't real good rawhide. Your dairy stock hide is thinner, and there's a lot of strength in your thinner hide." It takes ten or twelve feet of string to make one of Shorty's long buttons.

When Shorty isn't working with rawhide, he runs three hundred mother cows and claims the economy doesn't allow him to get any bigger. He used to lease three hundred and twenty extra cattle and another ranch, but it wasn't paying, so he turned the cattle and ranch back to their owners. The Prunty Ranch comes with sixteen hundred acres of deeded ground and he has permits to run on land owned by the Bureau of Land Management and the Forest Service. "The bureaucrats run them by the dates instead of the weather, and that doesn't make any sense," he mutters. "It always makes me cuss."

Cattle are fed on the home ranch in winter because Shorty believes it's a waste of money to move them, shipping out and back. "We keep them all here.

It's not too tough living up here. We have a beautiful house and TV sets with a dish that brings us a hundred channels. The phone usually works and the mail comes up every Tuesday. And we go to town about once a month."

Shorty has two sons. One works in the mines, and the other is a carpenter. "If they liked it, they'd be here. This place is a little dull for young people." One ranch hand feeds livestock in winter and helps Shorty year-round. Sometimes two cowboys work in summer, but Shorty always leads the horse drive to and from the Diamond A Desert. He often carries a thirty-five-foot braided lariat that he made. "It's a very short rope, so you have to be riding a fast horse!"

From the porch where Shorty does most of his braiding, it's a short walk to the barn where several skins await the cutter. "Oh, God," he sighs, "I wish I had these all twisted up into reins. I come and look at all these deer hides and I just about walk away."

OUR BOSS

He started young and he drifted far—
The owner out at the Diamond-Bar.
He has cattle grazing on many a hill,
But down in his heart he's a cow-boy still.

Though other owners put on airs,
It's little for style that our boss cares;
He wears his boots and his leather chaps,
And everybody calls him "Tap."

He bandies jokes and exchanges news,
As he rides the range with his buckaroos;
He sits his horse with a careless grace,
And rides at a stockman's jogging pace.

But the horses he rides all come of a breed
That are bred for mettle and built for speed.
The thing that he really most enjoys
Is a horse round-up with a bunch of boys.

It's then he rides at a pace that kills,
Through the open flats and the rugged hills;
With spurs set close and with flying reins—
Like he rode when a boy on the Texas plains.

Or else, when he jumps big mountain steers,
That have dodged the round-up for several years—
Down comes his rope, and away they dash,
While the hoof-beats ring and the cedars crash,
Till the bellowing steer on the mountain side,
Proclaims the fact that he's roped and tied.

I have seen him riding at racing speed—
Singing in front of a mad stampede—
As calmly as most old gentlemen do,
When sitting at church in a rented pew.

If he did retire and settle down
He would waste away in the sheltered town
Where he couldn't hear the cattle bawl,
The horses neigh, and the coyote's call.
He was raised on the range, and there he stayed—
One of the boys of the old brigade.

Bruce Kiskaddon

JEFF SAILORS Hitchin' Hair

This Montanan threw away a steady job to work with horsehair.

After tedious hours of counting and separating horse tail hairs, Jeff Sailors produces masterpieces of hitched art.

A Colorado native who prefers country farther north, Jeff Sailors is a handsome man, solid, with blue eyes and bushy beard. He helped build steel power lines for seventeen years, but then he decided to move to Montana and earn a living as a horsehair hitcher. A peculiar choice, he admits, "but I got tired of throwing my body to the wolves."

For twelve years he searched for an expert to teach him the hair-hitching art. Finally he found an old fellow who had spent time in the Montana State Penitentiary. Jeff knew that some fine hitching had come out of the territorial prisons, and Montana inmates continue to put out spectacular work.

"There's a couple of real famous guys inside who are generous with their knowledge," says Jeff, who has lived in Belgrade, Montana, for several years. "They are teaching whoever wants to learn. The guy who taught me was Jesse Stevens. He showed me a simple diamond design, which is what everything comes from." Jeff copied the basics from Stevens. Then the grandson of a Canadian Cree woman, a hitcher who had passed down her craft, showed him intricate patterns, which Jeff slowly turned into unique designs of his own.

His favorite hair comes from Mongolian ponies and is shipped from China in three basic colors: black, white, and mixed (which includes black, white, gray, and some brown). "The white hair is dyed to get bright, vivid colors," he says. "The mixed hair is bleached to a blonde color and then dyed to achieve more muted, earthier tones. The loose hair is then knotted and twisted into seven- to ten-hair strands." These strands are called "pulls." Jeff hitches or weaves the pulls around nylon or cotton cord, which forms the "warp." To achieve different patterns, craftsmen use a half hitch and a back hitch, adding different colored hair, and dropping out background hairs.

Hitched items look like tubes at first, so flat work like brow bands, belts, and spur straps have to be soaked in water and then pressed and dried between pieces of heavy metal. Leather ends are sewn on the ends of belts. Items like quirts and reins, which are supposed to be round, are hitched over a round core—rawhide for a quirt, rope for a pair of reins.

When hitching, Jeff is pulling, twisting, dyeing, and designing patterns. It takes him about an hour to do an inch of hitching, with extra time needed to finish the ends with leather or knotting. His most common designs include the diamond and the zigzag, also known as a chevron.

Learning the basics of horsehair hitching from a man who had been a convict at the Montana State Penitentiary, Sailors soon developed a style of his own.

Jeff, who has researched his craft, says he believes the use of horsehair for clothing and horse gear dates back to the Moors who conquered Spain in the eighth century. Spaniards brought the craft to the New World when Cortez introduced the horse in 1519.

Hair was used in the Americas long before the Spanish came. "The Indians used horsehair for everything from basket making to bridles," he says. "Sashes of flat, braided dog hair were found in early Colorado sites, and ropes

made from buffalo hair were found in Texas—all dating pre-white man. The Navajos used horsehair for ropes, cinches, quirts, and bridles."

Cowboys continue the tradition, mostly to make reins, quirts, and hobbles, but they also hitch hat bands, stampede strings, and inlays for saddlebags and chaps. Jeff adds, "Horsehair ropes couldn't be thrown very far on account of their lightness, so they probably weren't used as much as leather or rawhide ropes."

*Hitched-hair belts
are good looking
and long wearing—
as long as you don't
strike a match too
close to the hair.*

Braiders often debate which hair is best for horse gear. Some use hair from the manes of work teams, roached (or shaved) in spring and saved in sacks to hitch in the winter months. Some braiders take hair from their own cow ponies, although they are unlikely to be Great Basin buckaroos, who traditionally refuse to ride a shaved horse. Some prefer long-haired mustangs and hair of natural colors. Others like to dye the hair for a broader choice.

"Traditionally, there were three basic ways to work horsehair: twisting, hitching, and braiding or plaiting," Jeff explains. "Ropes were mostly twisted. Bridles and quirts were hitched, and belts and hat bands were either hitched or braided."

Twisting hair requires help. While the rope maker feeds out hair from a stack of tangled hair another person twists the hair with a gadget similar to an old-fashioned egg beater. Hair braiders use from eight to twenty strands, sewn together to make flat straps. Because of the complicated method of knotting, a hitcher can be imaginative and create beautiful and intricate designs. Jeff has a company called Gray Bear Horsehair Products. He hitches for nine months a year.

"I probably average sixty to seventy hours a week until summertime, when I take three months off and go to the high country and forget about horsehair." Which is not exactly true, since he always takes hair in his saddlebags when he packs into the hills.

Jeff is artful in his use of color. He has made bridles of black and turquoise hair. He has meticulously hitched bridles made of natural colors, which he prefers, such as beige, brown, and cream, including headstalls with fancy brow bands, tassels and a throat latch, reins and a romal. He has used yellow, red, green, mauve, cornflower blue, and violet. And he's probably the only hitcher who likes to switch bridle colors from one side to the other. Where a diamond is mostly dark on the left side of the headstall, his opposite diamond is mostly light.

"If I were to do this for fifty more years, I wouldn't run out of ideas for new designs and patterns. That keeps the long hours spent hitching from becoming boring." It also helps that Jeff's sisters are involved in cowboy crafts. His younger sister Jennifer makes saddle blankets that match his horse jewelry. His older sister Vickie is a hair braider and hitcher, taught by Jeff.

He likes the freedom that comes with his work. "One of the best things about hitching is being able to load all my tools and hair on a packhorse and take it with me to the hills," he says. "In fact, I seem to get more done in the mountains than I do at home. I'm only occasionally interrupted by native cutthroat trout rising to an evening hatch in one of Montana's pristine alpine lakes."

TRIBUTE TO AN HONEST OLD PONY

You can sing of Nancy Hanks,
Or the mighty Man O' War,
Praise the fame of Twenty Grand
And a hundred thousand more
That have galloped on the speedways
In a brilliant racing meet,
Or have trotted in the harness
To win a record heat.

But their fame is just as fleeting
As the scurry of their pace;
Soon another bunch of horses
Takes their places in the race.

But there's one old wicked pony
That will never, never die,
He will buck along forever
Scrapin' corners off the sky.

He was sired by Curley Fletcher,
Hard Experience, his dam—
He'll be comin' down the home-stretch,
While mere horses also ran.
When the others are forgotten
He'll be chargin' on alone,
This super-salty pony,
The old Strawberry Roan.

Gail I. Gardner

MARK DAHL Changing Times

When he lost his ranching gold, this optimistic Nevada cowboy

switched to silver.

Kate, an old Arab mare, shows off one of Mark Dahl's fine, hand-engraved, in-laid silver bits. This bit took about sixty hours to make.

His father and brothers all ran cattle on the grassy summer ranges that hug the Ruby Mountains in northeastern Nevada. They lived the good life. But when the cattle business soured several years back, things got tough for Mark Dahl. He was working on a ranch for his brother Demar and running a few cows of his own, but there was not enough income to support his family.

So the six-foot-six, bespectacled Mark started hauling barite ore from Stormy Canyon to Deeth. "I wrecked a couple of trucks, and that didn't work out too good," he says. "So then I went to silversmithing full time."

It was 1982. Mark Dahl had never seen anyone engrave on silver, and there were no "How To" books to be found. He had no background in painting, sculpture, engraving, or the art of silversmithing. He had little money. Even so, he hocked his house trailer and his cows and bought a few pieces of equipment. Some worked, some didn't. But Dahl is persistent (his wife Cora Lee calls it optimistic), and he went deeply into debt to learn how to make handsome and useful gear for buckaroos.

"I knew how to weld good," he says, "and to make bits and spurs you need to know how to weld." He took a jewelry-making class at Northern Nevada Community College in Elko. He pored over jewelry-supply and gunsmithing catalogs.

"I would never have had the guts to get into this business if I'd known what I was getting in for," he says. "This has been a very long and expensive education in my little shop. I was very naive."

In his early days of creativity, Mark got tips from Kenny Ramone, a man who made bits and spurs for Garcia, the most famous silver engraver, when the company was in Visalia, California. "I never met Ramone, but I talked to him on the phone a time or two and asked him advice."

Working mostly for Great Basin cowboys, Dahl kept practicing, improving with each piece, making bits and spurs, conchos, three-piece buckle sets, and horn caps. Today he makes saddle silver. He'll add new rowels or jingle-bobs to a favorite spur. He particularly likes trophy buckles and horn caps, "because you've got a lot of country to engrave on."

What makes nice engraving is a clean cut, and when the cut is very smooth and shiny with a mirror finish, it's like a cut stone. Most of the silver-mounted

Mark Dahl's work-shop is a tiny shack at the back of his house in Starr Valley, near Deeth. Here he's working on some rodeo trophy buckles. "I like buckles and horn caps," he says, "because I've got a lot of country to engrave on."

*Close-up of a
Dahl bit. Note the
Nevada star cheek
piece with silver
domes and inlaid
stripes.*

pieces sold in the United States come out of Mexico, where labor is cheap and the work is done fast.

Mark says some of the imported work is good, but much of it has chatter marks. "It looks as if it's just gouged in there and doesn't reflect any light. Most of the buckles are stamped out, not hand engraved." Fortunately, his customers appreciate the difference, too.

"I'm dealing with a narrow populace, especially in bits and spurs," he says. "The people who buy my work know the difference between stamped work, low-quality work, and fine engraving."

Mark always inlays the silver, even though overlaid silver is easier and cheaper. When he puts stripes on spur edges, he digs out the steel with a hacksaw or uses a mill bit on a drill press and routs it out. Then he fills the holes with sterling silver.

Sometimes he pours the silver. "I have melted it like it was braising, and that works good on a small area. A large area is more difficult because when silver melts it goes into a ball like mercury." The temperatures have to be just right—silver melts at seventeen hundred and thirty degrees—for a smooth

Cavalry-style bit, commonly known as a U.S. bit. This one also has a U.S. mouthpiece with a copper cricket.

flow. He heats it with a torch. "It doesn't change color. You just kinda get a feel for it when it's right."

He designs and builds custom horse gear. Sometimes a customer will sketch a piece, and Mark will redraw it to scale. After they estimate the amount of silver and agree on the price ("I just sorta guess at how much there is"), he makes the piece.

Mark's machinery is expensive, although most of it is secondhand or homemade. "The tumbler cost the most," he says. "Spurs and bits have to be smooth, very smooth, and the tumbler rubs and polishes them."

For years he has cut conchos by hand, but he recently bought a $1,000 die for the most popular two-inch size. He learned to cut by trial and error. A wood bandsaw went too fast to cut steel, so he took the motor out and put in bicycle gears. He added a drill with variable speeds to make parts. He uses a torch that cuts steel but leaves it rough; then he grinds the steel with stones and discs. He uses a bandsaw to cut spur rowels and a belt sander to shape and smooth them.

He uses a wire welder, and his bandsaw has the very latest blade. "There's

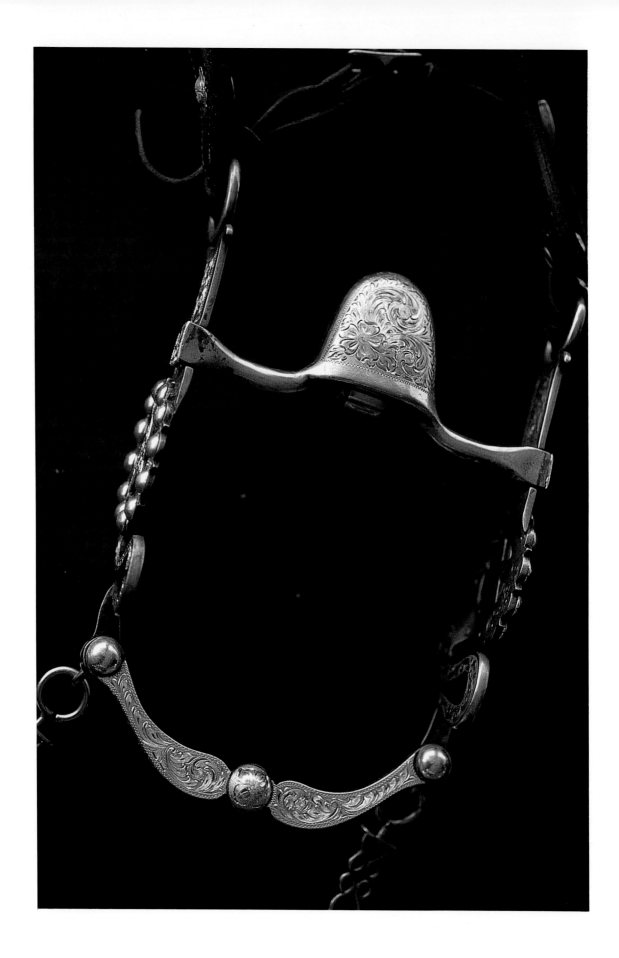

really sophisticated equipment out there, including computerized lasers. The cost of that kind of equipment would put me out of business."

To help relieve his debt, Mark accepts repair work. He once fixed some spurs with a big problem—they were too quiet. "A feller had a fancy pair of spurs," he says. "The rowels had silver inlaid in them, but they didn't ring. He had me take them out, put in rowels that I'd made with jinglebobs, and now they ring." He makes his jinglebobs from brass welding rods because silver wears out, he says. "Brass is better."

Buckles are usually silver or ten-carat gold on brass. "In some cases the gold is jeweler's bronze," Marks says. "Gold tarnishes and it doesn't take much to get expensive." Imported stamped silver is generally cast brass with electroplated silver or gold on top. "It's really pretty," Mark says, "but if you use something like that, the precious metal will soon rub off."

Silver is forgiving. If you screw it up, Mark says, you can melt it down and start all over again—"and you can't do that with steel."

Mark is always looking for new customers. He lives in Deeth, forty miles east of Elko, so he doesn't get any off-the-street business. Instead, he relies on the buckaroo grapevine. He sometimes gets contracts to make spurs, bits, or buckles for rodeos. Once he got an order from a fellow who didn't pick up the work.

"I took a $50 deposit for a $300 pair of spurs. I got the spurs ready, but the cowboy couldn't find the rest of the money." He sympathizes. "Things can be really rough in the livestock business. When nobody's got any money, that makes it rough for me, too."

The Dahl home sits on sixty rocky acres. Mark built the house with fence posts. He began with eight-foot untreated posts and had a sawmill cut them flat on two sides so they were five inches thick and would stack up even.

"The house is basically a rectangle, but it got to looking like a slaughter-house, so now it's got twenty-eight corners in it," he jokes. The house took five years and three chain saws to build. The floor joists are telephone pole cross arms. The banisters are made from peeled and dried willow branches fit together in a Mark Dahl design. The floor is laid with cedar two-by-fours he got from the railroad after a flatcar on a train coming through Deeth caught

Some of Dahl's fanciest bits are engraved outside and inside, including the steel, the copper hood, and the slobber bar.

Double-sided concho, identical and pretty from both sides, hanging in the middle of slobber chains.

fire. Half of the car was unloaded to put the fire out, and the two-by-fours were scattered all over the brush. "I bought them all for $500," he says.

To decorate the fireplace, which is the house's main source of heat, he used petrified wood found in the Ruby Mountains. Furnace ducts weave throughout the house. He made a stove for the kitchen out of a tar barrel. Keeping the house warm is a job in winter. "The upstairs is built looser, and when the fire goes out and the wind blows it's healthy up there."

The wood plank walls in the bedrooms are vertical, diagonal, horizontal. "He tongue-and-grooved each of them," Cora Lee says proudly. "He fixed the windows so I don't have to go outside to wash them."

Mark works in his shop from about six in the morning until after supper. He breaks to eat, feeds his few cattle, and does other chores. Until they were

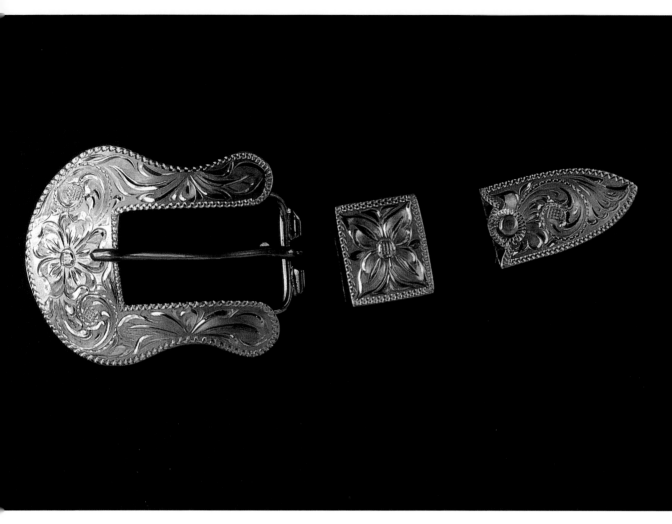

Three-piece buckle
set, ranger style.
These are available
in sizes from large
(for a one-and-a-
half-inch belt) to
miniature (used on
quarter-inch watch
bands).

old enough to go to Wells Junior High on the school bus, the Dahl children—Marianne, Thelma, Olivia, Enoch, Tabor, and Ammon—were taught at home by Cora Lee, who was born on a ranch in nearby Starr Valley.

Mark admires many great artists who work with silver, among them Mark Drain, Chip Darouche, Gary Gist, and Al Pecetti. They know that the type of gear horsemen want will depend on its use and where they live. "Texas and Midwest people use very simple bits and spurs; they're not anything like buckaroo spurs," Mark says. "Typical Texas would be overlaid, not inlaid. Overlaid is easier to do because you're not removing any steel to put the silver in; it's just soldered on there with a low-temperature solder." Inlaid is always more intricate; custom engraving has ten times as many cuts as stamped work.

The buckaroos of the Great Basin like spurs with big rowels. "It's the area

covered that's important," Mark explains. "A waterbed covering the floor is heavy but it can be set up on paper cups because of the large surface area that it covers. That's the same principle with a spur rowel. If you've got a little one-inch rowel with ten points on it like arena spurs, that small rowel with small points is touching a small area. But with a big rowel—say a three-inch rowel with twenty points on it where the points are close together—when it rubs the horse it feels nice and smooth."

Mark once corrected a pair of spurs that had only eight points on huge rowels. "The guy had me change them because they were too severe. He had me put more points, and smoother, so they would not be as hard on the horse."

Underneath the engraving block in the workshop sits a pan. When Mark cuts pieces off the sheets of silver, they fall into the pan. "Someday I'll burn my shop down and have a silver mine!" he says with a laugh.

The silver he uses on bits and spurs is 20-gauge sterling, which is probably less than one-thirty-second of an inch thick. His conchos are built on a base of either sixteen-gauge bimet or nickel. The base is strong, hard to bend, and doesn't corrode. The engraving is done on the outside layer of sterling silver. That makes the concho stronger, and it's cheaper because there's not so much silver in it."

Cowboy gear is closest to his heart, but for quick cash he makes jewelry such as bracelets, pendants, and earrings. "Unfortunately, I can make twice as much money per hour with a heart on a chain as I can with a spur."

Most of his work is custom-made or one-of-a-kind, but a few consignment pieces can be found in western shops. His bits run from $250 to $1,000 or more, depending on the amount of silver and gold and the complexity of engraving. Spurs run from $250 to $800 a pair (add $335 more for hand-tooled leather straps with large silver conchos on one side and miniature three-piece buckle sets on the other). His trophy buckles start at $175.

Experience in the livestock industry has helped Mark understand what works for certain cowboys and what works for a horse. He knows that the bit has to balance, that its surface cannot be rough.

Mark Dahl's work is beautiful, collectible, and useful. He says, "I guess if you want to poke a horse you can do that with a stick." But Great Basin buckaroos wouldn't hear of that. They would rather wear a pair of Mark Dahl's inlaid silver spurs that sing when they ride.

AND AS I RODE OUT ON THE MORNING (excerpt)

They decked him down with boots and leggings;
They decked him up with vest and hat;
They geared him out with all the riggings
A cowboy needs to make his tack.
The cantle curved high on his saddle;
The horn was anchored to hold cattle
On his riata of rawhide;
The swells were for the pitching ride.
His bridle of remuda colors—
The gray, the sorrel, chestnut, black—
Were from the fancy braided tack
Of various and sundry fellers
Who'd come to join a cowboy band
And failed to ever make a hand.

The boots and leggings had been Charlie's.
He'd wandered West from Arkansas.
The vest and hat were Jingle Farley's.
He'd gone back home to see his ma,
And, like so many another youngun
Who couldn't hack what had to be done,
Left ev'ry cowboy thing behind,
Discarded all that might remind
Him of his days out on the prairie.
The saddle was Black Jim's; he froze
In one bad winter's blowing snows.
His rope had hung Red Poison Berry.
Some braided reins had once been Ed's;
He thirsted out of broken legs.

They handed him a string of horses
With all the hues of Joseph's coat
And tracing from the blooded sources
Of old Pegasus' faunch and gloat.
And our Bellerophontes mounted
His winged steed and proudly counted
The labors that before him lay,
And measured works to fit each day.
And such were his days in the saddle

The prairie goddess smiled on him
Till sometimes it seemed seraphim
Were riding with him herding cattle.
In fact, such were his grace and skill,
Some jealous god might wish him ill.

Young Billy, mounting in the morning,
Hairpinned the horse in one smooth glide;
Then horse away and boy adorning
Became a centaur all in a stride.
He stayed the sunfish and fence rowing,
Stayed all the bronco tricks for throwing
The peelers who climbed on their backs.
They quickly came to him those knacks
Some rode for years without possessing.
Uncanny aimers seemed to guide
His looped riata of rawhide.
And this: he had his pardners' blessing.
Young Billy always seemed to find
The right place horseback the right time. . . .

He tarped some sougans for a hot roll
And laced a warbag out of hide,
And cut a scabbard for his pistol,
And belt to strap it by his side.
He rolled his bunk out in a corner.
No joiner, nor was he a loner.
He wisely plied the middle ground
That kept a reputation sound
Where talk was cheap and silence golden
Where private matters were concerned.
He heard his calling, and he earned
The label of a true and bold one.
They told the best of him—just this:
"He'll do to ride the river with."

Buck Ramsey

D. W. FROMMER The Hard Way

There are a thousand better ways to make a living than by making

cowboy boots, but this Oregon boot maker's craft has become religion.

D. W. Frommer was born in Detroit in 1946 and schooled in the Iron Range of Minnesota. But DW was born lucky—he had relatives in the West.

During his fifteenth summer he stayed at his uncle's ranch in Lander, Wyoming. He learned how to ride, discovered space and cowboy boots, and went back to Minnesota wearing tall-top, fancy high heels. "And I guess that's where I stayed, in my head—out West."

When his mind's made up, DW doesn't set a darned thing loose until he's got it right. He served as a paratrooper in Vietnam and was trained as a machine gunner. After serving in Southeast Asia he went to college for a while— "There's not a big demand for machine gunners in society, you know"—but school didn't work out, and he moved to Colorado.

While visiting his folks in Minnesota he met a midwestern girl named Randee, who later became his wife. DW told her stories about the West, and eventually they hitchhiked out to Eugene, Oregon. "We decided we liked Oregon," he recalls, "so we went home to gather together what poor possessions we had. Then we packed them into an old station wagon and came back."

They picked fruit to pay rent. Then DW worked in a foundry, and Randee worked in an art studio. As a Vietnam vet he was able to apprentice as a shoe repairman in Springfield, Oregon. Afterward, he found a job in a tiny town called Harrisburg, and it was there he met a saddle maker named Carl Portwood. "Carl's brother had been a saddle maker, his father had been a saddle maker, and they were pretty famous in John Day, Oregon."

Then DW met a mentor who pushed him in another direction. "Right after Carl died, an old man came down from Albany looking for him, and he stopped in my shop." The old man was Colonel Frank Finch, another saddle maker, and DW apprenticed with him for three years. But DW had not been raised a cowboy, and Finch, a man as intense as his student, insisted the saddle should be made for the horse, not the rider.

"I didn't have that intimate knowledge," DW says, "and I had a driving interest in footwear and the artistic possibilities of making boots. A saddle is a saddle, you just see brown leather. But boots . . . you see red, yellow, fuchsia, and chartreuse." DW changed direction and spent almost a year in Billings, Montana, working as an apprentice with Mike Ives, a boot maker.

*This intense and
talented boot maker
shows a two-tone
lace-up with the
bound finger-hole
that he developed.*

That was 1975. DW had already taught himself the basics of shoe making by taking shoes apart and rebuilding them. He used a geometric-pattern system that he now uses to make packers (laceup boots). But, he says, "I wasn't making a western boot that was worth talking about. Ives is the guy that taught me boots."

Ives said he'd seen worse than DW's work. It was pretty crude, but Ives admired his determination. "Well," Ives told DW, "I'm going to set you down with a baseball bat, and every time you make a mistake I'm going to hit you upside the head." Later, Ives offered DW a job, but DW turned it down. He returned to his family in Oregon and opened a shop on the main street of Redmond.

DW is still in Redmond, and he makes boots the old way, much as they did in seventeenth-century Europe. He doesn't use plastic, paper, or nails and is proud of that fact. His work might cost more than that from another custom boot maker, but he says he believes two things. "One, if you value your stuff low, the public will value your stuff low. Two, if you're not making at least a decent living on what you're doing, you're not going to be doing it for long."

He knows some custom-leather workers who try to price their goods low to compete with commercial outfits, but that doesn't make sense to him. "One old boy in Arizona is old and cranky, past his prime," DW says, "but his boots start at $900. He's making money at it, and he knows he's getting paid well for his work."

DW says virtually all commercial boot makers use plastic and nails, "and I'd say maybe 90 percent of custom boot makers use some nails, somewhere. It's simpler to use nails than to hand sew and peg, and it's cheaper." To hand sew around the welt and shank takes an extra twenty minutes per boot. To wooden peg each layer on a heel adds another four hours per pair. Sam Lucchese, one of the world's great boot makers, often said that when his father started in the late 1880s, they never used a nail. DW has looked at the whole boot-making operation, from making to repairing, and decided to do it the old-fashioned way. He says, "I've discarded everything that is built-in obsolescence."

DW's fame has spread, although he claims he has more of a reputation than he really deserves. Recently, a fellow flew in from Hawaii to order boots

because DW will not accept mailed-in measurements. Because of his pickiness, not only are his boots guaranteed to fit, they also are guaranteed to be made the old way, to be perfectly finished with details that can barely be seen. He uses a hand tool, which he believes dates back to the Middle Ages, that rolls around the edge of the rand beneath the heel to dress it up. He waxes the bottom of the boot until the sole shines so well it can be used as a mirror. Most customers don't know why they like a pair of boots, but they respond to details, he says. "It's a decorative thing, and I detail everything," he laughs. "It's something subliminal."

He uses all kinds of skins, usually in subtle and tasteful colors. He seldom blends more than two skins or colors. He muses about values and harmony.

DW's own red and black peewee boots. Hard to make, these three-piece boots, including one-piece top, have a single seam up the back. The four-part kangaroo-hide edging at the top of the boot, cut and beveled by DW, took eight hours to braid. (Photo courtesy D. W. Frommer)

Taupe full-quill ostrich vamp; dark brown kidskin top with taupe kidskin inlays. Careful beveling of the inlays ensures smoothness. "High dress boots should have white piping at the top," DW says, "for a pristine boundary." These boots took 150 hours to make.

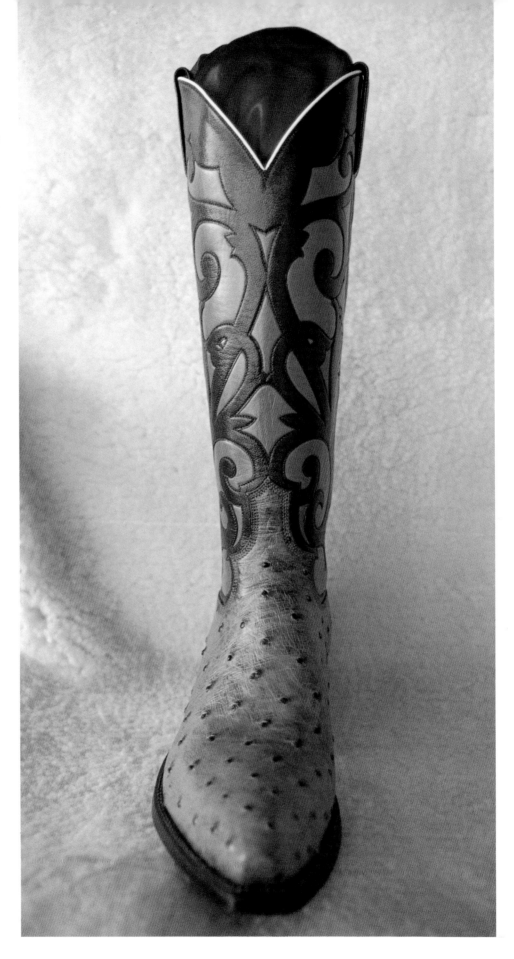

When he uses buttercup ostrich on the bottom with a dark quill point, he picks up that dark color in the stitch or as a color up on the top. When he uses an alligator vamp, he might add a matching top and pull accents. "That way you have harmony running all the way through the boot."

He takes great care to shave the edges of the leather when it joins another piece so there is no lump. "It shouldn't be clumsy. The surface has to flow." He looks for design but is just as conscious of the medallions of clear leather outside the stitching. "The clear leather has to make just as much sense as the pattern outline," he says. And the stitching has to be lined up "bing, bing, bing, bing."

Fanatical about detail, DW doesn't claim to have much artistic talent. He does a new pattern that's distinctly his about once a year, and he is impressed when other boot makers come up with new, attractive patterns and new ways to cut a top regularly. "A student came into my shop who had seen a lizard on a rock. He sat down and sketched this lizard with the tail curling around, with flagstones under it, and by the time he got done it was one of the most gorgeous patterns. It was aesthetically perfect. I just don't have that kind of talent, that's all. Never have."

DW says that many of his techniques go back to 1603 and can be documented in literature. For instance, he makes a thread out of nine cords of hemp or linen yarn and waxes it with pine pitch. "Originally they used sperm-whale oil, but now it's just pine pitch- and beeswax-based." He puts a taper into it and tips it with a boar's bristle that is plaited into the end of the taper. "It becomes a needle, and that really is the foundation of the boot."

Cowboy boots are normally made in four pieces, but DW makes quite a few from two pieces. "Up until about 1874, cavalry officers wore a two-piece boot which had a lower heel. It really was the two-piece Wellington boot." He says the military had a problem procuring quality boots. The soles would fall off, so the soldiers would go to local shoemakers to have duplicates made. "A lot of the cavalry officers' boots that we have today in museums weren't original issue. They were remakes from the civilian makers. And that's really where the western boot came from. The first example of a high-heeled boot made for a cowboy is a two-piece boot." The one-piece top, in vogue in the

1930s and 1940s, is pretty difficult to make. DW charges extra for a one-piece, "simply because of the extra work."

Inlays also are time-consuming, DW says, but some boot makers don't pay enough attention to them. "If an inlay is done correctly, every piece that is cut out of the leather is placed in behind the cutout after the inlay is done. That raises everything back up to the original level again."

It takes him about thirty to forty hours to make a pair of boots. D. W. Frommer boots start at $425, but a customer could spend thousands.

He says the hardest part is not in making the boot but in fitting the last, which is the solid wood shaper (or form) for the shoe or boot. Some boot makers measure the foot and take three-eighths inch or a quarter-inch off the measurements, but that's smoke and mirrors, he says.

"Arbitrarily taking off three-eighths of an inch doesn't speak to the fact that there are feet that are flabby, feet that are bony, feet that are muscular, feet that are fatty," DW fumes. "All those different feet can only be sensed through the tape measure. If you can't learn to take the tape measure and pull it just to the point where you compress the foot the way it's going to be when the blood has been pushed out of the foot by being in the boot; if you can't get a snug fit without chasing wrinkles ahead of the leather, ahead of your hand; if you can't do that, then you had better go back to school to learn how to do it!"

Master boot maker Cosimo Lucchese experimented with making plaster casts of feet, spending about $20,000 in the thirties but never got the system to work. Other well-known boot makers also tried plaster, but DW says it doesn't work for him. "Feet swell up if you sit around for a long time. A plaster cast will not tell you anything about how much blood is in the foot."

If a client is worried about fit, DW makes a Fitters Model, more common in the East and in Europe than in the West. "I build a real rough boot, a throw-away, and the person tries it on, and we test the shell that will be formed over the last. Then they might say, 'DW, you gotta give me a little more room over the instep, or in the toe area, or it's too loose here.' I'll go back to the last and modify it and rebuild the mockup so the fit will be perfect."

Old-time boot makers used to get defensive if another boot maker showed up at their store. They would cover their work so their secrets weren't passed down. DW differs in that approach. He has written a $50 book called, *The*

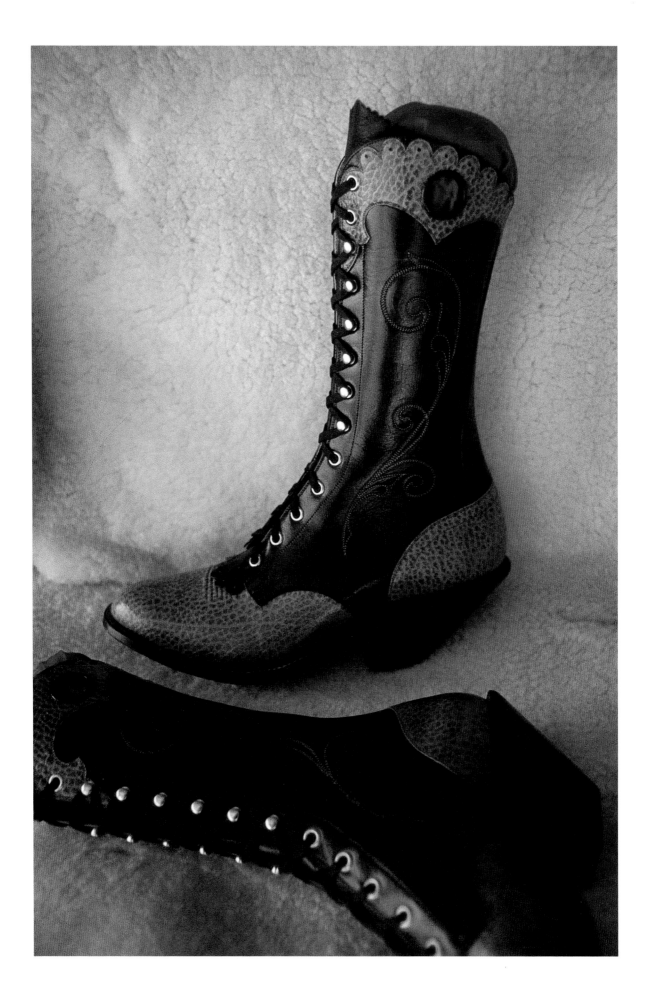

Making of the Western Boot: American Traditions. He also has a $200 version, intended as a primer, that includes patterns. "You can sit down, and if you follow the book step by step, you could make a pair of boots." He also has a twenty-seven-hour videotape, for $1,250, which includes the book and patterns.

Unlike most boot makers, anyone who has helped DW ("even anyone who's been congenial with me") can share his patterns. Some boot makers make a short counter (heel stiffener), but DW likes 'em long. He says, "It is generally accepted from Italy to Germany to England to America, that the longer the counter, the longer the heel stiffener, the more stability you'll build into the boot." If the stiffener is too short, the boots can be uncomfortable; if it's too long, it destroys the lines of the boot.

The heel base's length is usually one-quarter the length of the boot, but DW makes it longer. "I deal with Great Basin cowboys, and they generally ride the narrower stirrup, oxbow typically, and they come in and say, 'Keep the shank short and the heel long.'" DW says buckaroos want to get their foot all the way into the stirrup, which is where they like to ride. They don't do a lot of posting, and the stirrup leathers are not pressed up against the front or leg of the boot, rubbing a hole in the boot. Also, if a horse bucks and they get hung up, it's safer because the foot can be pulled free more easily.

He tries to keep a certain number of his boots within a cowboy's price range, because a good pair can cost a month's pay. It's always been that way. "At the turn of the century a fancy pair of boots would run $40, and a fancy saddle would run $50. The cowboys got paid a dollar a day during those times. A good saddle today costs $3,000, a pair of fancy boots $1,000 maybe, so, compared to saddles, boots have really come down."

The relative cost of boots recalls a story told by Sam Lucchese, whose father, Cosimo, was the premier boot maker in the Southwest in his day. Sam once got a boot order from a West Texas sheriff. The sheriff, a customer of long standing, said, "You've got my measurements." Sam looked in the records and saw that the sheriff's last pair of boots cost $95. The price would have to be raised. When Sam sent the boots and the bill, he expected to receive a complaint.

The sheriff did think $125 was a hell of a lot to pay for a pair of boots, but he sent Sam a letter. "I bought my first pair of boots from your grandfather, and I got to thinking," he wrote. "When I bought those boots I sold a cow and a calf, and it cost every penny to buy the boots. Today I sold the calf, bought the boots, and I've still got money in my pocket."

Another art to boot making is understanding leather. Skins come from all over the world. Ostrich is raised in South Africa, iguana and sharkskin comes from Mexico, python is from Indonesia, crocodile and kangaroo originate in Australia, and anteater is South American. Each skin is different. For instance, lizard is thin, which makes a dense, dry leather.

"The lifetime of lizard skin is anywhere from five to ten years before it starts cracking," DW says. "It's really pretty, and I use a lot of it for toe caps and heel scabs, because a lizard boot almost always cracks in the folds on the foot."

When DW buys colored leather, he buys skins that are "struck through," which means the color is saturated through the leather and doesn't just sit on the surface. Such skins don't cost more money, but they are harder to find. "People buy some boots and wear jeans, and they'll find the colors rub off and it's white underneath. You have to ask for skins that are "struck through" specifically, so if you scuff the boot, it's going to be the same color in the scuff as it was on the surface."

Quality is everything to D. W. Frommer, who insists he's not in the business to make money. "This may sound really egotistical—and obviously money's part of what I do, it's my living and my career—but I'm in it to make boots. It's almost a religion. You do the very best you can, and if you don't, then why aren't you a gas-station attendant, or a doctor, or something else. Because, if you are not doing it for yourself," he adds, "there are certainly a thousand other ways to make a better living than by making boots."

This master maker's work has been shown at the National Cowboy Hall of Fame in Oklahoma City, at the Cowboy Poetry Gathering in Elko, and at Wignall Museum in Rancho Cucamonga, California. DW was commissioned to make a pair of boots for the opening of the Gene Autry Western Heritage Museum in Los Angeles. He has been a featured artist at the Trappings show in Flagstaff, Arizona. He exhibits his work often, saying it keeps him stretched. "That's the thing that keeps you in there. As long as you are reaching, as long as you are just on the edge of what you possibly can do, you're still growing."

NEW BOOTS

I got my new boots and they fit me jest right.
Of course all the other hands sez they're too tight.
Some sez they're too small, and some sez that they figger
They're shore big enough, but my feet's a heap bigger.

Last night a dumb waddy was springin' a joke,
How I pulled the tape measure so tight that it broke.
I've got the Lumbago—the hands all got cute.
Said I ruint my back pullin' on my new boots.

The boss sez the heels is too high fer his likin'.
Well he shore ort to know I don't use boots fer hikin'.
They fit me jest perfect. The tops is stitched fine
The boss's boots never was e'kul to mine.

I ordered them boots and I paid the cash down
And they's no better boots in the country around.
I know why them fellers won't let me alone.
When they look at my boots they're ashamed of their own.

Bruce Kiskaddon

FOREST FRETWELL

Makin' It Work

For a fancy bit and spur maker, this Idaho cowboy has a strange

preference for old iron.

Forest Fretwell's spurs have seen some long miles in the saddle. These are the first he made, when he was fourteen years old. Even though he has fancier ones hanging in the house, he prefers to wear these "because they're just a part of me."

The old headquarters of the Gusman Ranch was close to Jordan Creek Bridge, a few miles out of Jordan Valley, Oregon. Forest Fretwell's grandfather owned the ranch and a big stone house on the hill overlooking the entire valley. Forest's father died before he was three, and his mother brought him and older brother Carl from Arock, Oregon, to the family ranch.

"It was granddad Gusman's place," Forest says, "and he raised us here."

By their twenties, Forest and Carl had bought out their grandfather. They had a quarantined herd when they started, and brucellosis took a lot of cows. "We lost two hundred and fifty right off the bat," Forest says. They went broke but managed to save the ranch.

The brothers leased the land to pay off the debts. They looked for work. Forest managed a ranch in the Klamath Basin. He was gone for nine years and got married young. "I was just a big kid," he says. "I was twenty-one and Nancy was twenty." The Delamar Silver Mine had opened a few years before he left, and the local population doubled to four hundred. There were jobs available. Carl continued to live at the ranch and worked at the mine. When the title was clear the boys borrowed from the bank to stock the ranch with their own cattle.

Today the Fretwell brothers own thirty-six hundred acres, barely enough for two families. But they work extra jobs to help pay the debt. Forest, who runs a feed truck part-time, also works as a silversmith.

Forest has been making horse gear for a long time. He made his first pair of spurs when he was fourteen. His first bit is hanging on the wall inside his house, "and it sure could use some improvements."

The bits he makes are usually Santa Barbara style, with large cheek pieces. He makes his own dies, everything from scratch. He designs, modifies, and cuts his own patterns from old Spanish bits. He uses copper for patterns because it's thin and can be laid on the steel and cut. He works in overlaid silver, some inlaid, and does the engraving too. Some steel he bends cold, other parts he heats. He always tries to build spurs to a person's liking.

"A long legged person will probably want a bigger rowel so he'll be closer to his horse. I custom make it, know what I like. If they ask me, I'll tell them. Otherwise I'll build what they want."

Fretwell moved to his grandfather's homestead in South Mountain, Idaho, when he was three. His old spurs were made in 1954; the fancy new ones, based on the California Spanish style, were made for Butch Brown of Jordan Valley, Oregon. Brown's include loose silver disks on the rowels.

Cheek pieces and a slobber bar from two identical bits, being made for Jack and Joe Doan of Nampa, Idaho.

opposite:
Close-up of overlaid silver bits, showing hand engraving and raised jeweler's-bronze brand, the Slash H.

He makes half-breed bits and all sorts of spades, but he also makes snaffles and ring bits. "A ring bit puts more pressure on the lower jaw. It can be used by a horse that's been a good old bridle horse all his life that's got old and heavy in the mouth. If you use that ring bit on him, it'll pick him back up."

During the bicentennial year, 1976, Forest was asked to appear at the Smithsonian Festival of American Folklife in Washington, D.C. He remembers how he and several other craftsmen, including neighbor Frankie Dougal, set up stalls in the park between the Washington Monument and the Lincoln Memorial.

"We were in a barn made out of hardwood, fashioned after these old barns you see around here falling down. I had one corner of a shed, and a lady braiding rawhide was in another corner, and there was a saddle maker inside. It was fun—a lot of people come trailing through."

He fixes plenty of bits, some worn out, others broken. He points out a cowboy's cavalry-style bit that is missing some silver. "I'm going to fix it up so it'll look like new," he says.

However, Forest doesn't fancy up much of his own gear, preferring to use an old iron-jawed Santa Barbara bit. The bit has no silver, but the metal is engraved. His neighbors often joke about it.

"Hey, Forest," one old rancher called to him during a rodeer where they were sorting livestock near the Owyhee River. "There's a guy up on Jordan Creek who will probably put silver on that bit for you!" Forest just kept on riding, but shortly after that he retired the plain one and put his headstall and reins on one of his pretty silver bits.

"Guys were taking bets on Juniper Mountain that I'd never use a fancy bit," Forest laughs. "They said I'd used old iron ones for so many years that I'd leave it hanging on the wall. But I've used the silver one all summer."

Forest and Nancy have four children, five grandkids, and a handful of dogs and cats. He has received gifts for serving in several associations. One gift was a pair of spurs made by Elmer Miller, but Forest wears his own and hangs the gifts in the house. He has collected pieces of cowboy gear, including an old bit made by Stanton and Goldberg in Winnemucca in the early 1900s.

"I like it, but it's a little out of proportion for my idea of a bit. It's too short in some places, too long in others, and would put too much pry on a horse." He's made both heavy bits and light bits. "A lot of horses just won't pack a heavy bit. They try to spit it out, fight it and flip their head."

He has Mexican spurs that have been at the ranch all his life. He has a hair rope made by Helen Hammond, Frankie Dougal's daughter, and a beautiful Indian cradleboard made by Hazel Able, the chief's wife at McDermitt, Nevada. "We raised two kids in it. It works."

Forest has been invited to display at the Trappings of the American West show in Flagstaff, Arizona, several times. For that he always makes something special, intending to keep the item. But somehow, for cash, he can be talked out of it.

In the winter he works full time with the cattle, so he can put in only about four hours a day in his workshop. "When I first moved home, I was going into that shop in the morning and—if I didn't have a run on the truck and wasn't

Hand-engraved Fretwell spur with overlaid silver, sixteen-point rowel, and matching concho on spur strap.

working with cattle—I'd work from dawn until eight at night and never come out of it."

It takes Forest about thirty-five hours to make a bit by hand, despite a couple of disadvantages. One eye has only 18 percent of normal vision, and he lost a finger several years ago. "I goofed up this hand, got it caught in a machine, pretty near lost the whole hand." His fingers are stiff, so he grips his engraving tools close to the palm to hold them steady.

Forest likes cowboying the old-fashioned way, sometimes using a rawhide reata. "I've had one since I was a boy, and now I've got a little bitty one, not much bigger than a pencil, that I use on spring calves. It's like lightning when you throw that out and give it a little whip. It just sinks. It's not dead like one of those nylon ropes."

Outside their deeded ground the Fretwells run cattle on about twenty thousand acres of land belonging to the Bureau of Land Management (BLM). It's hilly country, with lots of junipers and rocky bluffs. It's where his grandfather started in the livestock business.

Forest looks across the icy creek to the cattle that are bunched up at the edge of the irrigated fields. Snow has covered the meadows for weeks, so the livestock has been fed from the ranch's own rolled meadow hay. There are about five hundred mother cows at the ranch today, besides calves, bulls, and horses, between the two families. Forest ponders the future, worrying about the lean spells that show up too often. He hopes that fish eaters and vegetarians will re-educate themselves about the values of red meat.

"If we can live with hard times long enough," he says, "I guess we are gonna be all right."

THE COWBOY

He was made in the West, where a man's put to test
By the horses and tracks that he's made.
And his love for the land is a thing that is grand.
Life's dues have been hard, but they're paid.

The lessons he's learned and the pride that he's earned,
And the knowledge that speaks in his eye,
Came from hours in the saddle while he's trotted astraddle
'Tween the land and the good Lord's blue sky.

Through the drought and the flood, he's bathed in life's blood.
Life and death seem the stones of his path.
He's seen Nature's death put the unfit to rest,
Or the love of a cow's newborn calf.

And he's been imitated till he's near constipated,
By the folks that are fakin' his part.
They can play till they strand, but they won't understand
That they're missin' what lives in his heart.

And he's got enough sense, to take down the fence
That corners most mortal men's mind.
He knows Mother Nature and sure won't forsake her.
She's twice as hard as she's kind.

And his God, as he knows Him, and the things that He shows him
Has taught him one thing for sure.
Mother Nature is hard, and you die what you are,
So friend, hope your tracks have been pure.

Leon Flick

RANDY STOWELL

Ultimate Brush Buckaroo

Horse trainer, rawhide braider, and hair-rope maker,

this Elko cowboy survives and thrives on the desert.

Randy Stowell has learned the value of time spent alone. He can braid rawhide, twist horsehair into mecates and cinches, and recite cowboy poetry. He spent his youth at the Stowell Ranch on the Bruneau River in northern Elko County, Nevada. After graduating from high school he learned to be a welder at a school in Utah.

But Randy missed Nevada's sweet basin and range. During one long winter more than a decade ago, he came home. His job was to care for several hundred cattle and a few dozen horses at the home ranch while the rest of the family stayed in Elko until the thaw.

Randy was alone for months. He fed the stock from wild bottomland hay that he and his brother had cut with horse teams the previous summer. He did chores, worked young colts, doctored the sick, fixed fence. It was always cold, often well below zero, and because of the towering red and white cliffs at the edge of the rocky river next to the ranch house, it was gloomy much of the time.

During that season, with the help of a Coleman lantern and a "How To" book by master rawhider Bruce Grant, the young buckaroo taught himself the basics of braiding rawhide.

"Braiding is time-consuming, tedious," he says quietly, tugging his long mustache. "The more you do, the better you get. The hardest thing is to make the braids smooth and even."

He worked the rawhide for hours at a time, because he had the desire, the time, and the hides. He had trouble with uneven strings. He says most old-timers used a board and pocketknife to cut the hide, "but it's not as easy as using a string cutter. I looked at three or four different cutters and finally designed and made my own."

Randy started tying rawhide buttons on the hair ropes known as mecates. He made small pieces like stampede strings and quirts. He made tassels and gave them away to other cowboys. After years of practice his work became exquisitely fine and smooth, and now he makes twisted horsehair ropes and cinches, rawhide and leather reins, hackamores, bosals, hobbles, headstalls, and reatas.

"I prefer a rawhide reata," he says, "but very few cowboys have them anymore because nylon ropes are stronger and easier to use. A nylon rope can take

*Randy Stowell,
a creative Great
Basin buckaroo,
with his bold mus-
tache and wildrag.*

the jerk where a reata can't." While the average nylon rope is thirty to thirty-five feet long, Randy's rawhide rope measures close to seventy feet. A rawhide rope is strong but difficult to handle. The cowboy has to use a leather saddle horn because a rubber horn won't allow the rope to slip, which can break the hide. "You need the length," he explains, "because when the cow hits the rope you have to let the reata run through your hand and slip around the leather horn. You can control how fast it goes by the pressure through your fingers. It's way harder to use a reata, but easier on a cow."

This working cowboy, long used to working with rawhide, also likes to work with the tanned hide of a kangaroo. "There's a lot of braiding going on in Australia, and kangaroo hide is the stoutest hide there is. When it's processed into leather, it's soft, real soft, and it's nice to work."

Randy's first set of kangaroo reins was sixteen strands, with a twenty-

strand romal. His first kangaroo bosal had a twenty-four-strand nosepiece. "I would class them as fancy," he smiles. "In the bosal there's around twenty-five hours of braiding time. In the reins probably about forty-five."

For several years Randy and his brother Gary have run cattle together on leased land, including the family ranch. Their parents retired and moved to Elko; Gary and his family of five now live in Rowland, and Randy and his wife Marvi and their two children live on a ranch near Currie. The brothers have slowly built their herd to five hundred mother cows, and they lease a hundred more from their father. Their cattle graze in winter in Nevada's central deserts and in the summer on the Bruneau River close to Idaho.

Running a cow-calf operation in a place of mean winters means the Stowell brothers have to raise hay to feed when the snow is too deep for the stock to find forage. Their ranch is so far from conveniences—roads, stores, parts, and gasoline—and has so many people to support, that air-conditioned, tape-decked tractors are not in the Stowells' cards. They hay with an ancient tractor and some antique equipment pulled by workhorses and mules. They stack hay with a pitchfork.

"The workhorses are usually part Belgian or part Percheron," Randy explains. "We break them, train them, and use them for haying. Eventually we sell them as work teams." Some ranchers have to feed in winter using a team because the snow's too deep or the machinery won't start. Other ranchers simply prefer horses to trucks.

With about one hundred head of horses at the ranch in Currie, Randy spends most of his time there. He finds enough material to make mecates and horsehair cinches from his own stock. "We would never roach the mane of a saddle horse," he grins. "A cowboy wouldn't want to be seen with a horse with no hair." He uses mane hair because it's softer than tail hair. It takes three or four hours, with help from members of his family, to twist the hair into a rope.

"But twisting the hair isn't all you have to do," he says. "To make a rope you have to 'pick' the hair first. And when you pick it, you have to get the hair ready to twist out, with all the strands going in a different direction. It has to be like a girl's hair that's ratted, a mess. So you have to take three or four strands of hair at a time and drop them in the box and that just fluffs the hair

Mohair cinch by Randy Stowell, in red, black, and white, with brass rings.

up and gets it all mixed up. That's a real slow process. It takes six or seven hours picking out hair for one rope."

Mecate makers mix colors for appearance and make ropes of different thicknesses for different uses. A heavy mecate, perhaps three-quarters of an inch thick, is used for starting a horse out because the big mecate is easy for the rider to grip. When the horse becomes better reined, a smaller mecate can be used. "Later, when you put him in a two-rein, you use a little half-inch or three-eighths-inch rope. He's lighter in the face then and it's easier."

If a hackamore is braided with too few strands, it can be coarse and chafe a horse's jaw. If the nose button and heel knot are not balanced properly, and if the bosal is not stiff enough, the horse can suffer. If a tail-hair rope is used as a fiador, instead of one made from mane hair, it can itch the horse's neck and

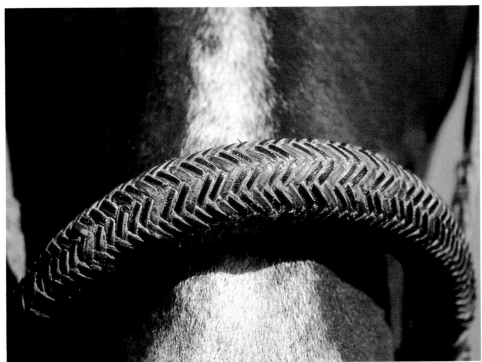

Leather bosal, braided over rawhide body. Leather (tanned hide) is softer on a horse's nose than rawhide (untanned).

below:
Two strands out of a possible eight, twisted, black over white, for the start of a pretty mecate.

drive the animal to distraction. Also, a heavier mecate teaches a young horse to feel and know what it's expected to do.

Randy Stowell will continue to train his teams and rope, brand, and doctor his cattle. He will always be ready to help his neighbors, most of whom live dozens of miles away. He will continue to recite cowboy poetry, as he has several times at Elko's Cowboy Poetry Gathering. And he will always be making something cowboys can use in horsehair and rawhide.

Even though this buckaroo is quiet and shy and prefers the open range to the middle of town, he knows he is involved in city folks' dream of the West. "But," he admits, "cowboying is hard work, long hours, low pay. It's not as romantic as everybody thinks it is."

For Randy Stowell, his work and art are not for glory. He is simply preserving a piece of his heritage the best way he can. To his delight—or chagrin, he's not sure which—he recently discovered he's about to be wrenched from the nineteenth century.

"Pretty soon," he grins, "I should have electricity and a phone."

THE PRIZE POSSESSION

What's the last thing you would part with?"
I once asked a cowboy pal,
Expecting him to answer,
"Why, that hoss in yon corral."

Or maybe, "That new saddle,"
Which he'd saved for years to git,
Or possibly his granddad's spurs,
Or that silver inlaid bit.

Or the fancy rawhide work
Hangin' in his saddle shed,
Or possibly his roping skill,
Or that pretty girl he'd wed.

A hundred things went through my mind,
From boots to cold, hard cash;
But the thing he promptly answered
Was, "This handlebar mustache!

"Took thirty-five long years, you see,
Ta finally get 'er growed.
And even though it's vain,
I like my old mustachio."

In his ancient quest, Diogenes,
With lantern in his hand,
Would've found his representative
If he'd stumbled on this man.

And there's hundreds out there like him,
On the western cattle range,
Who cultivate their facial hair
And ain't about to change.

Now the dang things are a nuisance
When winter time moves in,
And you've got two big, long chunks of ice
Hangin' way down past your chin.

And in a while your cold red nose
Will start to run and dribble,
And before you get your mittens off,
That freezes in the middle.

Boy, your napkin gets a workout
When the menu's soup or stew,
And it sometimes gets discolored
From tobacco if you chew.

There's the slow recovery period
When she's singed by brandin' fire,
Or when wife with maddened viselike grip
Should demonstrate her ire.

Or you're maybe shoeing horses,
And this bronc sets up a clamor,
And a handlebar gets hung twixt claws
On the downstroke of your hammer.

There's the, "Ooh, that tickles, Honey,"
When the ends get nice and long,
And you have to readapt your style
Of talkin' on the phone.

Oh, the trials and tribulations
Of the man with the mustache
Are just the dues he has to pay
To possess a bit more dash.

To receive those looks of wonder and awe
From the kids with peach-fuzz lip,
And the fascinated looks from babes
Who reach and grab ahold of it.

But they say it's really worth it,
And you feel that you've come far
When you see that dashing buckaroo
In the mirror behind the bar.

Oh, sure, you'll hear some whispers,
And those out of range make cracks.
But just straighten up, take out the tube,
And add a little wax!

Joel Nelson

JEAN SPRATLING Hookin' Wool

Latch hook rugs, an ancient folk art, have turned into spongy, comfortable

saddle blankets for equines in the Ruby Mountains.

Weaving a saddle blanket is hard work for Jean Spratling. It hurts her neck and back. "I can't do it very long," she admits. "I usually sit on the floor, lean back against the couch, then loop the wool through every other hole, hooking it through."

Jean's hard work, though, pays off in soft, comfortable saddle pads. Her blankets are soft and bubbly. She has made blankets for Christmas presents, for her husband Craig, her father-in-law, Max, and friends. A few have gone in the bottom of her kids' cradles, soft and warm, thick and strong.

When the Elko County rancher started making blankets, they were plain, all one color. Then she experimented with stripes, later adding brands to the corners. But her creations have remained what they were meant to be—saddle blankets for the working rancher.

Working her material, she uses her finger as a measure for tension on the wool as she loops it, but that technique doesn't work for everyone. When she taught a friend over in Clover Valley how to make blankets, her friend's came out too tight.

"I don't know what she did, but she told me if I wasn't charging $200 for these, I was crazy."

It takes Jean ten hours to make a plain blanket and twenty to make a fancy one, but she charges only about $100 and it costs close to half that for material. She explains, "I don't figure cowboys are going to pay much more than that."

This gentle woman, wife, and mother of four children, lives in Starr Valley, Nevada. The family's large house is shaded by tall cottonwoods and silver maples and is surrounded by cattle. The view to the south is of the Ruby Mountains. To the north is their winter range in the Snake Mountains.

Jean's mother, who was born in Cedarville, California, was a rug maker who learned how to make saddle blankets from an old neighbor, Ernie Archer, from Alturas. Ernie used wool from his own sheep, and he cleaned and prepared it himself. But when Jean's mother found a place to buy "top" wool— wool that is ready to spin—Ernie was happy to quit cleaning his own.

Jean gets top wool for about $7 a pound. It is available only in black and white and comes in long strands. Jean divides the strands into thirds so it's the right thickness to pull through the loops. She then rolls them into balls to make it easy to work.

These latch-hook blankets, showing initials and a brand, have been used hard and vary in age from four to eighteen years. The old one used to be white and was made by Jean Spratling's mother, Betty Cockrell, as a wedding present for Craig. The blanket is still in use. The five-year-old brown and white with the "Lazy E on a Bench" brand was made by Jean, for Craig.

Pure, thick wool blankets, good for the horse, easy for the rider. The M Slash J blanket was made for Jean's in-laws, Max and Joyce Spratling. Max uses Jean's blankets, but this one is displayed in the ranch house.

The top wool Jean uses is the best she can find, but the Wisconsin company that she prefers no longer offers black. "It has to be high-quality wool with really long staple," she says. Lately she has been using dyes to add more colors. She tried turquoise and red, but the result was closer to pink, so she continues to experiment.

She used to sell saddle blankets through western shops in Elko such as the Eddie Brooks Saddlery, but Eddie moved fifteen miles south to Spring Creek, and now she says she can't keep up with requests from her friends. "We're so busy on the ranch, I don't make enough to put in the stores anymore." She teaches friends how to loop the blankets but not many of them stick with it.

"It's tiring," she says. "It takes a bit of muscle to pull the wool through right. They got frustrated."

The quality of her saddle blankets has been tested by hard use at home.

Available colors of
top wool are white
and brown. Jean
has been experi-
menting, dyeing her
own to offer more
choices. "Unfortu-
nately," she says,
"my red dyes have
been turning pink."

Her husband Craig has had one for ten years and still uses it. "This blanket breathes so the sweat doesn't stand right next to the horse," he says. "Wool absorbs the sweat a bit more."

Jean's saddle blankets measure about thirty by thirty inches and are two inches thick. Blankets from Mexico are sometimes made of wool but are so thin that riders have to use an extra saddle pad, "and synthetic pads aren't near as good as wool for the horse," she says.

Craig's father, Max Spratling, moved to Starr Valley in 1962 and bought a ranch in the shadow of the Ruby Mountains. Jean and Craig moved to an adjoining ranch in 1982. Together Craig and Max have acquired forty thousand deeded acres and permits on an equal amount of BLM ground. Most of the range lies north of Interstate 80 in the mountains north of Wells. Their summer range borders the Winecup Ranch, formerly owned by the Utah Con-

struction Company and actor James Stewart. The Spratlings run about sixteen hundred mother cows, and they feed three thousand head, including calves, bulls, and horses, when they are off the range.

The winter process is fairly automated, with Craig feeding from stacks, using three or four different machines. "One of them slices hay off the stacks with a sickle," he explains. "Another has a big grapple fork on it, like a backhoe." Feeding is usually finished by ten a.m., but he feeds calves a second time in a feedlot at about seven at night. The rest of the time Craig works as ranch and farm mechanic, fixing machinery.

In summer Jean takes care of the ranch's vegetable garden. Year-round she helps the children, driving them to 4-H and basketball games and taking them the twenty-five miles to Wells. She helps with branding, sorting, calving, feeding, doctoring, and other necessary chores. She also keeps the ranch books.

Meanwhile, Jean continues to hook her luxurious wool blankets, and, according to Craig, is a darned good roper.

"Ranch work is hard," she sighs, as she hooks another blanket, "but as hard as it is, I'd rather be sitting in the saddle than be working with wool."

ALL DRESSED UP

Things is pickin' up as most folks knows,
So I sent to town fer to git new clo'es.
Some onderwear and a big hat box,
A couple of shirts and a passel of socks.

Some overalls and other truck,
Three red bandannys throwed in fer luck.
My boots ain't new but they'll do right well,
I reckon I'll make them last a spell.

I'll be the pride of the whole derned spread
With a fust class Stetson on my head.
A bran new slicker tied on behind—
It's strange how yore clo'es improves yore mind.

Nice new clo'es purtects the hide
And sorter contents a man inside.
Clo'es does a heap toward makin' the man.
Try goin' without and you'll onderstand.

Bruce Kiskaddon

LARRY SCHUTTE Cow Boss & Twister

This intense buckaroo remembers the bad times and labors for good.

Standing ramrod straight and wearing a flat-topped, stingy-brimmed hat, Larry Schutte impresses even the casual observer. This intense buckaroo was raised on an outfit near Twin Falls, Idaho, where his family ranched, farmed, and ran a feedlot. He's a mix of German, Irish, and Cherokee.

Larry Schutte (pronounced "Shooty") is cow boss of the Quarter Circle S near Tuscarora. Owned by the Van Norman family, the ranch has twelve thousand deeded acres and over fifty thousand acres of BLM land where they are allowed to run livestock seven months a year. The cattle are turned out on the public domain in the middle of April and brought back to the home meadows each fall.

When Larry left a ranch near Battle Mountain to come to northern Elko County as cow boss, he didn't know the country. "As far as your feed," he explains slowly, "you got to notice your feed in your lower country and use it first 'cause it's goin' to dry up first."

He tilts his head and squints. "As far as your waters, you just watch your cows and they'll teach you where your waters are. When you run outside cattle that come from California, you pretty much have to get around to see where your feed is and lead them to the right place. You have to utilize the range properly. You have to put your cattle on at the right time of year, or else it dries up and they won't use it."

His position at the Quarter Circle S is "about a three-man job." Larry and his wife Toni do most of it, with extra help hired for weaning, haying, and the roundup. Toni often calves the cows, and Larry thinks she's perfect. "Toni knows what's going on. When it ain't done and it's got to be done, she just takes care of it. She was raised that way, on a ranch."

Larry, who is on occasion a reciter of buckaroo verse, belongs to a breed long forgotten. He is a man whose path is now straight, whose dreams are secure. His talent for making perfect horsehair mecates is, he believes, God-given.

He learned about horsehair mecates in 1979 from his neighbor at the Spanish Ranch, Bill Kane, "a rope maker deluxe." Larry admired Bill's strings, and when Bill gave him a rope, Larry studied it for quite a while. His admiration was so great that today he finishes his ropes by pulling the braided end through four times, just as Bill Kane did.

After the mecate is twisted, Larry has two people help him tie off the ends in a "turk's head" or "monkey's fist." Sometimes the knots are covered with braided wool, sometimes braided rawhide.

"Picking," or preparing the hair for twisting, is a skill in itself. Schutte piles criss-crossed horse mane hair on the floor about two or three inches deep, then takes the hair and rolls it up in a bun. "That makes it easy to feed the strands of hair out to make a string," he explains.

If the hair is slick, Larry finds that it feeds out easily. "It has to be even and consistent, 'cause to make a rope come out pretty your strings have to be right. Same as rawhiding—your finished product is in your strings." Good rope makers can pretty much guarantee the strings they twist are all the same size. "If the string width isn't consistent, with big spots and little spots, the rope's going to have bumps in it."

Larry is so talented at making rope that he doesn't seem to be paying attention while he's working on one. "It's in the hands," he says. "You get to where you can do this by feel without looking at it." At the home ranch he has two trailers, end-to-end, fitted with all the machines necessary to make ropes, including one of only two in the country that picks hair.

"That rig that can pick hair was built by a cowboy, and we can pick rope in about an hour instead of four hours."

No self-respecting cowboy would roach the mane of his own horses, so rope makers have to learn of sources by word of mouth. Hair is hard to get. Some is coarser than others, some is dryer, just like human hair.

Hair costs about $1.50 a pound, Larry says. "We can't pay more than that due to preparation time. You get too much in it, and a lot of hair that's shipped to you has weeds, trash, blood, cockleburs, and it takes too long to clean it. Then you can't make a dime on the rope."

He will, however, pay more money for clean, pretty-colored hair. If hair comes dirty, he washes it by hand "because," he laughs, "it's pretty hard on washing machines."

When he's not working cattle or twisting horsehair ropes, Larry writes poetry that often turns out to be "kinda irky, anti-government. I get to writing something on the wild horse situation and it makes me upset so I get on the hook and I don't like to. I don't let anybody read it. All the propaganda about wild horses in the movies! Horses in the movies were fancier than anything I've ever seen. Walt Disney made them sonofaguns equal to Pegasus. If you

could just expose what these horses look like! The last bunch we gathered were so inbred they dropped to a six-hundred-pound average and had crooked legs. They were sick and dying. It's against human nature. Are we going to let 'em bunch up like rabbits until disease kills them and then they'll have nothing? In some places in Nevada they are like rats in the big city."

Larry admires cowboy poet Bruce Kiskaddon, and his recitations of other poets' work are memorable. Larry's poetry may be hidden away at the ranch, but his ropes are not, and he's constantly learning. His ropes are tight but not stiff. He pays attention to the weather and points out that too much humidity will make a mushy rope. "Some old cowboys like a soft rope, but if you have a rope with a lot of life, you don't have to pick up the whole rope to send the message to the horse's face." Simple wrist movement can move a Schutte rope, which is valuable for experienced horse handlers and for horses that are sensitive to hand action.

"Feel how tight that is," he says, offering one of his ropes. "Try to untwist it. We put such a mash on those strings this one direction that they want to stay in the opposite direction. That's what makes the life in the rope."

As he twists the ropes by machine, Schutte tests the tightness of the string to determine the twist, or life, in the rope. He usually makes six-strand ropes, but fine finished work often has more strings in it.

"If you wanted a big old crude rope you could just have a couple of large strings, and they'd darn sure be stout," Larry says. "You could put ten real small strings in there and it would really be a pretty rope, but if you put a lot of twist to it and make it too tight you stand more chance of popping those strings."

He is famous for a rope that is extremely tight when new, but he says, "After about four rides your hands will take off that stickery stuff and it'll feel real good." Toni advises that if you want a softer rope, put it in the washing machine.

The entire family is on the payroll of the Schutte Mecate Company. Toni helps twist the ropes, and their kids John and Reata help to pick and clean hair. (John is learning to make mecates, and Reata plays a mean fiddle.) In the past few years Larry has added a stamp to the ropes so people know it's one of his. "Some people try to make certain knots in the end, to make a white

Before making a horsehair mecate, the craftsman has to "pick" the hair, strand by strand, and roll it into buns. These, in sorrel, gray, white, and black, are ready to twist into strings.

tassel in the ropes, or build their poppers in a different way for identification, but there are so many people doing it that it's hard to tell whose is whose. I've heard—not that my ropes is any good—that some people in other states are taking Mexican-built ropes and trading them to people, saying they were Schutte mecates."

He doesn't take orders for ropes anymore because, he says, he's married to a thousand head of mother cows. "I don't like the pressure of having orders and people wanting them," he says. "I might have to do something else."

When he gets to town, which is seldom, Larry doesn't wear a fancy wild-rag like other buckaroos. "Why don't I? I dress the way I need to for my work. When I go to town, I'm tired of wearing scarves all the time. Tuscarora is where the storms are made, where it's cold. I wear lots of clothes. Sometimes I wear two pair of pants and longjohns. It cuts the wind, you betcha."

There was a time, several years back, when Larry spent too much time in cowboy saloons. It was hard on his family. He forgot one entire evening when he apparently drank for six hours, tried to drown himself in a mud hole, then talked about whipping a bunch of his buddies. "I'd lost my mind," he says. "I had a cup taped to my hand, a drinking cup, because I just kept dumping liquor all over everybody, dropping the glass." Because he didn't remember it, he got scared. He figured he could really hurt somebody, so didn't drink for a long time. He prayed and asked the Lord into his life. "Now I have a personal relationship with Jesus," he says. "He's your partner—he's right there. We talk to him every day. He guides us in our daily work. We've prayed over this house. It's full of angels watching this place."

The family runs fifty of their own mother cows along with the main herd as part of their wages. And they earn extra income from selling mecates and Toni's hitched-hair work. "If we were to get right busy we could invest in cows or machinery that we could borrow on. There's no expense to rope making and hair hitching, really, and we can do the work when it's dark. Time is the expense."

Larry enjoys rawhiding but it's tough to make money on it. "Rawhiding takes a lot of time. The weather here inhibits you from working hides because of the moisture. The hides won't dry out unless we bring them inside. You need

For a rope, the art is in the strings. They must be made with constant diameter and tension. A Schutte rope is famous for uniformity. If a rope is used a lot, the projecting hairs will soon wear off.

to prepare all your hides in summer, cut the hair off, and cut them in strings. Then you can soak them and put them in a sack in the house and temper them down. You can do that at night."

The Schuttes obviously enjoy each other. There is a peace in the family. Larry doesn't expect anything from God. "I'm just thankful. I don't look to Him to do anything more. I'm thankful He's not just putting the wrath on me, thankful He's given me all these blessings—wife, kids, dogs, get along with people. Amen."

Forty-eight horses were brought out to the desert for a four-day cattle drive. Buckaroos choose a fresh mount every day, and spend any spare time they can find training green colts or shoeing their horses.

THE COWBOY'S SOLILOQUY

All day o'er the prairie alone I ride,
Not even a dog to run by my side;
My fire I kindle with chips gathered round,
And boil my coffee without being ground.

Bread lacking leaven' I bake in a pot,
And sleep on the ground for want of a cot;
I wash in a puddle, and wipe on a sack,
And carry my wardrobe all on my back.

My ceiling the sky, my carpet the grass,
My music the lowing of herds as they pass;
My books are the brooks, my sermons the stones,
My parson's a wolf on a pulpit of bones.

But then if my cooking ain't very complete,
Hygienists can't blame me for living to eat;
And where is the man who sleeps more profound
Than the cowboy who stretches himself on the ground.

My books teach me constancy ever to prize,
My sermon's that small things I should not despise;
And my parson's remarks from his pulpit of bone,
Is that "the Lord favors those who look out for their own."

Between love and me lies a gulf very wide,
And a luckier fellow may call her his bride;
But Cupid is always a friend to the bold
And the best of his arrows are pointed with gold.

Friends gently hint I am going to grief,
But men must make money, and women have beef;
Society bans me a savage and dodge,
And Masons would ball me out of their lodge.

If I'd hair on my chin, I might pass for the goat,
That bore all sin in ages remote;
But why this is thusly I don't understand,
For each of the patriarchs owned a big brand.

Abraham emigrated in search of a range,
When water got scarce and he wanted a change.
Isaac had cattle in charge of Esau
And Jacob run cows for his father-in-law;
He started in business clear down at bedrock,
And made quite a fortune by watering stock.

David went from night herding and using a sling
To winning a battle and being a king;
And the shepherds when watching their flocks on the hill
Heard the message from heaven of "peace and good will."

Allen McCanless

EDDIE BROOKS

Sweet Music, Stretchin' Hides

Living in the last of America's big country, working sure but slow,

this master saddle maker runs half a decade late.

Eddie Brooks talks slowly, and, it's nice to say, he makes saddles that way, too. Even though he may be two or three years late with saddle orders, when someone comes into his workshop, he stops to visit. He offers coffee, puts a huge wad of snoose in his cheek, and enjoys the conversation. He spits in a can, sometimes contemplating how far he has come from his early days "piddling with leather" in Texas.

His family ranched when he was little, but they moved to town when he was about nine years old. Soon after that, Eddie's future was assured.

"There was a guy who lived a little ways from us who done leather work," he drawls. "He wasn't a saddle maker, but he made billfolds, purses, and belts, so I got to hanging around and picking up his scraps and messing with 'em."

The first thing he made was a belt. He had seen one in a Montgomery Ward catalog and tried to copy the design. He cut the leather with an old bolt that was sharpened on the end, using it like a swivel knife. "Well, it didn't swivel," he chuckles, "but it served the purpose, you know. I made the background with an old Shinola Polish bottle filled with red stuff made from a bunch of Texas wild berries." The hardware for the belt cost him $5, which was what he eventually sold the belt for.

After high school Eddie cowboyed and rodeoed a little, riding bareback broncs and bulls. "Bareback horses was my best lick," he says slowly, "and I didn't have too good a lick on any of 'em. But I rode 'em best I could." He also hung around saddle shops until he finally joined Leddy Brothers, one of the West's greatest, at The Stockyards in Fort Worth.

He stayed for seven years, until 1964, when he moved his family to Nevada so he could work for Capriola's, the western store and saddle shop in Elko. "I really loved Elko because it was really a cow town. This part of the Great Basin is the last of the big country." But his wife got homesick, and two years later they went back to Texas. Eddie returned to Nevada alone in 1975 and worked for seven more years at Capriola's. He opened his own saddlery in Elko in 1982 and moved his shop to Spring Creek in 1989.

Eddie Brooks doesn't make trees for his saddles or engrave the silver, but he knows how to pick what's right. Tuscarora buckaroo Pete Mori says, "Good saddle makers know where to get good trees and the importance of the tree to

This saddle, built on a cottonwood Ellensburg-style tree, was made for the author by Eddie Brooks. It has high swells and cantle, sheepskin lined tapaderos, and is decorated with brass studs and Brooks and Agee flowers. (Photo courtesy Jim Le Goy)

make it easiest on the horse. Eddie sure knows how to pick a tree. Eddie sure knows how to make a saddle."

When making the tree—the wooden foundation for the saddle—good saddle makers consider the type of horse and the rider, too. "You need to find out just what type of horses the people ride and the kind of riding they're gonna do," Eddie explains. "I kind of eye 'em up and down, talk to 'em and quiz

'em and really find out just what they want. Then I make suggestions that I think will work for them and that I know will work for the horse."

Eddie likes cottonwood for a lady's saddle "because it's light, tough, but not hard." For a man's he uses white pine and fir. The way the cowhide is used is also important. Eddie uses neck hide for the groundseat. "It's real thick leather, but it's coarse-grained with real big fibers, so it stretches and is not as strong." The fenders and seat will come out of the butt of the hide "because that is your best part of your leather, the most dense fiber, highest quality, and it's real tight grain on the rump." For stirrup leather he uses the back, which offers strong fibers that won't stretch much.

If he could, Eddie would make saddles only for cowboys, who understand what works and always appreciate a good one. In fact, about 80 percent of the saddles he makes are for working buckaroos, even though, ironically, they're usually the ones who can least afford them.

"People who really know saddles and use them a lot, well, they know what feels good, and I try to figure out what suits them. The way different guys are made, it makes a difference to what kind of seat. To put a good seat in a saddle, that's real important. You need to spend a lot of time in putting the seat in the saddle, skiving it just right, because the guys who ride 'em, they

opposite:
A slick-fork saddle is the type favored by Great Basin buckaroos. This saddle, made for "a very good hand," Elko cowboy Lanny Morrison, has fancy basketweave and flower tooling. It proves Eddie Brooks has a passion for detail.

A saddle is getting pretty close to ready when Eddie Brooks puts on the oil. This basketweave saddle took over 120 hours to make.

The basic tree for a quality saddle is made out of soft wood such as white pine or fir. The author's saddle was made of cottonwood because it's lighter than pine but still tough. Trees are shipped already covered with a heavy bull rawhide, which gives it strength. The gullet cover and front rigging goes on first. This saddle has a five-eighths single rigging. (Photo courtesy Roche Bush)

sit in 'em all day long." In cheaper production saddles, riders seem to sit on top of the saddle instead of down in it, "and that can sure make you sore."

It may be hard for most people to tell a good saddle from a bad one, but after more than thirty years in the business Eddie can spot a good saddle from two hundred paces.

He tries to teach young saddle makers a serious lesson. "I tell 'em, you know, there's a lot of stuff underneath you are going to cover up. If you take pains to do it good, if you be particular about it, it'll make the whole thing more particular. Then you'll be more particular about the topside, too."

When Eddie visits a ranch, the cowboys usually give him heck. "I was talking to 'em, you know, and I'd be pickin' these little old fuzzy things that were stickin' up out of their saddle that I thought should be trimmed off or sumthin'. It wasn't hurtin' a thing in the world but if they'll get that in their mind that every little thing from start to finish is important, that they should be real particular on it, it'll make 'em a whole lot better all the way, you know."

To make a saddle takes about forty hours for a simple, single rigging—plain, slick, or roughout. Brooks's base price is $1,900. With a double rigging

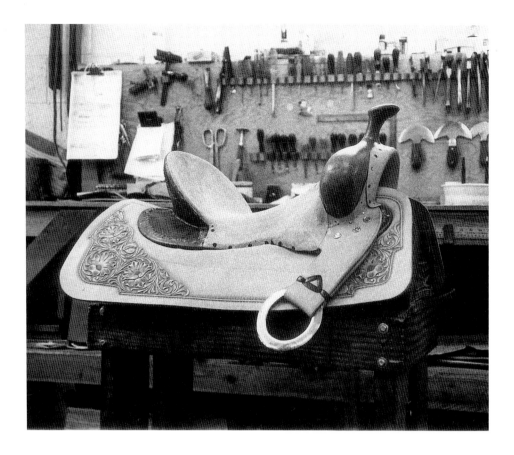

($130 extra), flat plate rigging ($165 extra), full basket stamp ($475 extra), or any intricate tooling job, the time can go up to three hundred or four hundred hours. "It just depends on how fancy and intricate you get. Of course, silvermounted will cost you more." He recently shipped a $15,000 saddle to a man in North Dakota. "It was just as good for the horse," he says, "but it had a lot of silver on it."

Over the years Eddie has changed a few habits. He used to keep horses in the yard, but now his pasture next to the shop is empty. "I got enough age that I don't feel like messing with young horses anymore. I just haven't got the time because I'm concentrating on my custom work."

Eddie is delighted when his customers are pleased with his work, but the ultimate compliment is when other master saddle makers offer their respect. If you ask a Nevada buckaroo, a Texas cowboy, or a hand from any other western state about the best of the saddle makers today, they'll probably mention Dale Harwood, Chuck Stormes, Duff Severe, and Don King. And, inside and outside the masters' saddle shops, Eddie Brooks's name comes up often.

He takes orders now for saddles he can't hope to deliver for years. The

*The reservoir is low
but the cattle are
thirsty so they have
to be pushed away
to get back on the
trail for a few more
miles.*

demands and pressures from buyers are sometimes hard, but Eddie under-stands. "You got to try to accept things. Sometimes it eats on me because I cain't get 'em out as quick as I'd like to. I know people wouldn't order them from me if they didn't want 'em. They don't want to wait 'til they're dead before they get 'em, you know."

He wishes he could work more quickly, but he refuses to compromise for speed's sake. "I'm going to take the time and do 'em right," he sighs. "I don't want to make every saddle in the world. With the ones I do make, though, I want to take the time to make 'em good."

COWBOY TIME

If Genesis was right on track concerning Adam's birth
    And seven days was all it took to build the planet Earth,
Then where does carbon dating fit? And all the dinosaurs?
    Plus all that other ancient stuff that happened on our shores?
Now, I believe in scientists. They aren't just lunatics!
    But I believe in Genesis, which leaves me in a fix.
The answer finally came to me while making up this rhyme.
    God made the earth in seven days, but . . . that was Cowboy Time!
Have you ever called the shoer to set aside a day?
    You scrutinize your calendar, say, "Tuesday'd be okay."
The big day comes, you take off work, alas, he's never seen.
    You call him back and he inquires, "Which Tuesday did you mean?"
Did you ever place an order to get a saddle made?
    An A-fork tree and padded seat with silver hand-inlaid.
As decades pass, all you can do is sit around and eat
    So by the time it finally comes you've padded your own seat!
A friend came by on July Fourth. He swore he couldn't stay
    But then he said, "For just a bit." He left on Christmas day!
"Soon," to all my cowboy friends means next year . . . or tomorrow
    Depending whether in the deal he plans to lend or borrow!
"A couple days," "a little while," "not long," or "right away!"
    Should not be taken lit'rally in cowboyville today.
But like I said, the precedent was set so long ago.
    The angels had to learn themselves what all good cowboys know.
They worried if they didn't work to keep the schedule tight
    That Earth would not be finished by the deadline Sunday night.
They'd never learned to think in terms of "rollin' with the flow"
    But God does things on Cowboy Time . . . to watch the flowers grow.
He bade the angels to relax and said, "For Heaven's sakes,
    I'll get it done in seven days . . . however long it takes!"

Baxter Black

HELEN HAMMOND Passing It Down

The third generation of Idaho hair twisters makes magic with rope.

It was New Year's Eve at the White Horse Bar in McDermitt, Nevada, when Helen Dougal met Carl Hammond. They danced all night. Later they wed, and Helen moved from her family's Idaho ranch to the Hot Springs Ranch near Golconda, Nevada.

Helen is a hair-rope maker, just like her mother and grandmother before her. She was only ten years old when she made her first mecate. She liked making ropes but stopped when she and Carl married.

"When I got to Nevada, I was discouraged," says the pretty, dark-haired Helen, now in her thirties. "I didn't have any horsehair, I didn't have the setup, I couldn't get going, and my two kids were babies."

Helen's mother, Frankie Dougal, wanted her to make ropes to carry on the family tradition. Her father, Chuck Dougal, brought down a rope-making machine similar to one he'd made for Frankie. Helen was inspired. She found more time when her daughters started school. She bought some hair and started twisting ropes, following her mother's patterns and enjoying what she thought was a dying art.

Dougal-Hammond ropes are distinctive, often striped barber-pole style. Helen says, "Mom and I are, I think, the only ones in the country who do them like this. I have seen mecates all over, but none of them ever struck me as fancy."

Mecates from Mexico aren't as strong, she says. "You can take them and twist them apart. Ours you can't. People buy Mexican ropes because they are $35. Ours cost twice as much." She adds, "I always feel sorry for buckaroos 'cause they don't make a lot of wages. That's who I want to sell them to, because they are going to use them."

Ropes are twisted by hand, to about twenty-one or twenty-two feet, and are used with a snaffle bit or a hackamore. To make a good bridle horse, cowboys often switch from a snaffle to a hackamore before putting a horse in a bit. "If you put a bosal underneath the bridle with a little hair rope attached," says Carl, "then you can slip from hackamore to bridle easier. It's a Spanish thing, to control them with that light bosal. You can still control the horse and don't pull on his mouth as much."

The machine that Chuck Dougal copied for Frankie and Helen was in-

The most popular mecate is five-eighths of an inch thick and eighteen or twenty-one feet long. The rope, used with a bosal, becomes a hackamore.

vented by Glen Walker in Owyhee. It enables one person to spin string, reducing time and labor.

"I can make three ropes in a morning," Helen says. "I can spin all the strings, then have two other people help me put them together. I make strings, eight of them, hooking them onto nails, then we twist four and four together."

Carl ties the Turk's-head (or turban-like knots) on Helen's ropes and takes care of the leather tails at the other end. Helen picks or sorts the hair and spins it with the machine. Carl and his mother Dorothy help Helen finish the ropes.

Helen's best seller is a candy-stripe rope that uses lots of black. It's tough to tell Helen's work from her mother's because they use the same pattern book, created by Frankie. Frankie, who knows the patterns so well she doesn't need to look at them, can go for weeks without repeating herself. Helen has some of her mother's ropes on the wall, "and they are not for sale."

Rope design, however, usually depends on what color hair is available. Helen makes sure she uses the best. "Pretty white, pretty sorrel, pretty black—I like to use distinctive colors."

Basic colors are black, white, sorrel, and gray, but there is great variety within each color. Some sorrel is dark and has black in it. "I call it a dirty sorrel," Helen says, "and it's hard to work up into pretty designs." Sorrel is most common, encompassing every shade of red and brown. Gray is rare, as

is good white. Helen often mixes grays in several shades and usually adds a little white.

"You don't come by those colors very often. There's always lots of black, lots of sorrel, lots of Hereford cow tail, which is white. I use cow tail if I have to, if I have no other white, because it adds a little color and brightens up the rope."

If she can't get enough white mane hair, Helen bleaches cow tail and treats it with Downy fabric softener before she starts to spin. "Cow tails are better than horse tail, which is prickly." After the bleach and Downy, she says, "they turn out pretty soft."

Helen still doesn't have much time to make mecates. Shortly after seven each school day she or Carl takes the girls several miles to the start of the pavement to catch the bus to school in Winnemucca. They pick them up each

Four of Helen Hammond's mecates, modeled on the neck of a white horse. Her favorite is barber-pole style, two color (white and gray) and four color (white, gray, sorrel, and black), learned from her mother, Frankie Dougal. Also shown here, white with black dots, and a plain black rope.

afternoon. After their ranch chores, both steal time for cowboy crafts and art. Carl draws and paints, makes bits and spurs, and engraves the silver on Chuck Dougal–made spurs.

In spring, when the calves are weaned, the fat ones are put onto pasture and the rest are fed at the ranch. Old cows are culled and the sick are doctored. Carl, Helen, and his parents do most of the work. "See that dust through those trees?" Carl says. "That will be mum and dad bunching cows right there. There should be about a thousand head."

Carl and Helen catch their horses to go out and join them. Helen, despite years in the saddle, admits riding makes her nervous. Even so, she likes to ride big horses in the mountains and deserts—and outrun wild cattle. "These horses have stamina. This horse has never given out on me, ever, and I've run him for miles. He's eight now, and I've had him since he was coming two."

Helen and Carl ride out to the desert from Hot Springs Ranch, which sits in a brushy flat not far from Interstate 80. Smoke from the stacks at the power plant at Valmy can be seen to the east. Mountains surround them. They are fifty miles from Winnemucca.

"I wouldn't want to move closer," Helen admits. "I couldn't stand it. Sometimes the kids lose a lot of activities at school because of our isolation, but they gain in certain other things out here. We are an hour from town, and that's a good distance."

NOON BREAK

When heel flies are buzzing and sun is real high,
I ride along trails where parched grasses sigh,
Where grasshoppers signal with crackling click,
The dust-devils swirl and I think I'll be sick.

My cinch is plumb loose from my pony's wet sweat,
For a swaller of water I'm starting to fret,
My skin has turned lobster from scorching hot rays,
And insects keep stinging—I've seen better days.

Then a silvery crick wends its way through some trees,
My horse needs no urging; we're both awful pleased;
I pile off and drink, take a gander around,
Then stretch out to rest on the toasty warm ground.

For some folks a luxury's a big fancy car
Or diamonds and yachting, but I claim by far,
There just ain't a thing that's near halfway so sweet
As a nap in a meadow when heat's got you beat.

Gwen Petersen and Jeane Rhodes

AL TIETJEN Gambling on a Greenhorn

It took a few years and a trip to California for this Nevadan to perfect

his craft.

"It was perfect," Al Tietjen says about his family's ranch north of Winnemucca, Nevada. The ranch supported four hundred head of mother cows and had twelve hundred acres under fence, but Tietjen's youth was spent elsewhere. "Dad was afraid he wouldn't be able to get help after the war started, so he sold the ranch and we moved to Reno in the spring of 1942."

Al Tietjen (pronounced Tee-jen) was about twelve when he and his two younger brothers started school in town. But on summer vacations the boys would be chasing cows on a ranch in Paradise, Nevada, owned by their uncle, Elmer Miller. After the chores were done, Al would spend time with Elmer in the workshop. They made bits and spurs by hand and got so good at it that Elmer decided to leave cows and range behind. He leased the ranch to his brother, and he and Al struck out for California. In San Francisco they found John Olson and Crete Haverland, who ran the Olson Oldie Saddle Shop. A silversmith named Raphael Gutierrez—who had worked for the famous silversmith and saddle maker T. S. Garcia in Elko in 1907—was making bits for them, and the old Mexican was more than willing to help the newcomers.

"He showed us a few tricks," Al says. "He told us how to put silver on the side of bits, how to do inlays, how to go in and chisel all the steel out, raise the edge up, and set the silver in there."

Hammers and chisels were their basic tools. With no competition from low-cost imports, they found that one good western store could keep them busy. "This kind of gear was 90 percent handmade at the time, and we were making a living at it, me and Elmer," Al recalls. "I was a teenager, and he was about thirty-five."

Their work was stamped Miller & Tietjen, and quite a few of those bits and spurs are still around. "Those first buyers were gambling on a bunch of greenhorns," Al laughs, looking at a bit he made in about 1946. "That's one of the first ones I ever engraved—and it looks like it!"

They worked in San Francisco for four years before returning to Reno around 1950. Shortly afterwards, Al was drafted and served two years in the army during the Korean War. Meanwhile, Elmer went back to Paradise Valley to take over the ranch. Later, Elmer moved to Idaho and started a bit- and spur-making school. Miller & Tietjen never worked together again.

Two styles of Tietjen bits. The top one is overlaid silver on a Sonora-style bit. The bottom bit is Santa Barbara–style, using inlaid silver on blued steel.

Al Tietjen uses a vice and a hacksaw to cut a cheek piece for a Sonora-style bit.

When Al Tietjen returned from Korea, he spent the summer visiting at Miller's ranch. He returned to Reno in the fall to work as a mechanic in a Ford garage, but he continued to make bits and spurs for friends.

Al married Elsie in 1954, and they moved to Smith Valley, Nevada. They raised potatoes at her family's farm, but Al didn't like it. "If I wanted to be in anything," he says, "I'd be in a cow outfit instead of spuds." They moved back to Reno, where he worked again in the Ford garage and then built swimming pools.

In 1968 Al returned to the work he loved—silversmithing. He started a stainless business, designing bits and spurs, making patterns for the dies, and manufacturing the parts in Los Angeles. He had patterns for eight different bits as well as for the bottom bar, the mouthpiece, and the rollers. When the pieces were ready, they were shipped to Fallon, Nevada, where Al supplied belt sanders and tumblers to Chet Smith and Dan Dockery to clean them up. Then, back in Reno, Al assembled the pieces.

As the distributor, Al placed his bits and spurs in saddle shops, feed stores, and western-wear stores, anywhere he could sell them. Until foreign competition came along, he did just fine.

"I couldn't whip the two-bits-an-hour Korean labor rate, which is pretty tragic." Ninety percent of the mass-produced items available today are made

A classic example of the California-style spur with solid button and drop shank. The chap guard is also common on Texas spurs. This is hand-engraved inlaid silver on blued steel.

Old, tarnished bit, overlaid, in classic California style.

overseas, in Japan, Taiwan, and Korea. Even India is getting into the business. Mexican craftsmen, under pressure from work quotas, have learned to produce pieces fast. A Mexican bit can wholesale for about $185 in the United States. Al says, "We sure can't compete with that."

During his best times, Al Tietjen mass-produced eighteen hundred items a year. Now he's back to custom work, making three or four items a month. "It beats shoveling ditch," he smiles.

Intricate hand-
engraved inlaid
silver bit with large
cheek pieces in the
shape of wagon
wheels.

When he gets some of his work back for repair, it's often unrecognizable.
A cowboy from Spanish Springs brought Al some spurs to change a hook on
the jinglebobs because they were sticking. "I couldn't even see the band or
anything on it—there was manure all over them, and mud." He wiped them
off, fixed the jinglebobs, and the cowboy was happy.

He's partial to good-quality steel, especially when it's polished out and
blued with a torch. The blueing can last a long time, depending on use. "If you

get fingerprints on them, wipe them off and it should be all right," he says. "There's acid on your fingers, and it can affect the color." He buys his silver in sheet form, and on inlaid bits uses pure silver. On overlaid bits he uses sterling.

"There's a 7 percent difference in copper between pure silver and sterling," he explains. "The pure is softer and easier to engrave and costs a little bit more. The reason you use pure silver is that when you go to blue the bit, pure will not change color."

If a flame is put on sterling, it will turn yellow, and even though it can be buffed, that causes problems. "It's just barely surface color," he says. "You don't dare touch the blueing with a buffer—it will come right off."

Blued steel turns brown with age. It can rust. But once the blue's gone, the bit can be oiled to prevent deterioration. "Dry it off good and then put a thin film of olive oil on it. Don't use WD-40 because it has kerosene in it. That's an abrasive and it will evaporate."

He seldom uses jinglebobs, which he calls "just another warning system." When a spur rowel starts wearing, it will jingle enough so a horse will know what the fellow is doing," he says.

Spurs take longer to make, so Al prefers making bits. "There's something about spurs," he says. "They irritate you a little more. You gotta exert a little elbow grease." He confesses, "I'll get a little wild once in a while, but I just walk away from it, go do something else, and then come back."

A pair of spurs his son John made in 1981 have been hanging in the living room for years. John did all the steel and silver work. He cut out the rowels and filed them down, then cut out the shanks and cut out the heel bands and heated them. There's no machine involved except a band saw. He put the silver in himself, and Al did the engraving.

"These are spurs that I taught my son to make," Al says. "I told him never to sell them because I wished I had the first article I ever made. I have no idea where it's at. It could be in a junk pile for all I know." One time when John needed $200 and wanted to sell his spurs, his father gave him the money and said, "Your first spurs are not for sale. They stay in the house."

The younger Tietjen is a steelworker and doesn't make spurs now. "I can't afford it," John says, "I'd starve to death doing this." His father agrees,

pointing out that if his son made a bit today at his labor rate, it would cost more than $1,500.

Al's work is used and displayed by cowboys and collectors all over the world. His name is so well known that most people think he must have died decades ago; but he's still fit, although his work has changed in the last few years.

"When I was manufacturing," he says, "I was selling fifteen hundred to eighteen hundred items a year starting at $150 apiece. Now I make three or four a month from $350. Now there's a difference!"

Manufacturers are pushing managers and workers so hard to mass produce that they don't take the time to put quality into the product. There are saddles on the market with trees made out of plastic and there are dies to stamp the leather. "The sewing on the saddle is just a big die that'll smack in there and they're producing them for $300 to $500 apiece." That's what tears up good saddle makers like Eddie Brooks, Scott Brown, and Reno's Bill Malloy because they can't get the price that they ought to. "People see these saddles and they think they're the same thing," Tietjen adds, "but I'll guarantee you that if they ever tied onto a fifteen-hundred-pound bull, they'd find out they weren't the same. They'd split right in half. The tree would go flying down the flat."

At his workshop just south of Reno, Al Tietjen spends a lot of time filling custom orders and repairing gear. He has a few samples of his early work, including a bit that got run over by a horse trailer. "You can't stop one place," he says, eyeing a piece that looked as if it was the work of a greenhorn. "You gotta keep going up hill."

BETWEEN THE LINES (excerpt)

Cow-boys in clothing tattered,
Faces and hands brush scarred,
Saddles and chaps all battered,
Horses look gaunt and hard.
The heat and the dust that smothers,
The tired out horse that lags,
The calves that have lost their mothers
Wailing along in the drags.

That's why I'm giving you warning—
There's something I cannot tell.
The joy's as clear as the morning
The torture's akin to Hell.
They never will reach outsiders
Who were raised in the town's confines,
But they're here for the hard old riders
Who can read them between the lines.

Bruce Kiskaddon

TIM McGINNIS Freedom & Choice

Enjoying the buckaroo way despite low pay, long days, and the caprice of Mother Nature.

Peacocks were used to keep rattlesnakes away from the bunkhouse and to announce visitors. This peacock just walked between a nose button on a two-rein hackamore and a portion of a rawhide romal.

There are peacocks strutting around the bunkhouse at the Twenty-Five Ranch near Battle Mountain, Nevada. "Martin Black brought them here when he first came to work," Tim McGinnis says. "They are supposed to scare away rattlesnakes."

Tim, who has been there three years, has become a serious believer. A cowboy who previously lived in the same bunkhouse told Tim there were rattlesnakes underneath the house, but no rattler has been seen since the strange birds arrived.

Tim has worked for several ranches as a rough string rider, jigger boss, and buckaroo. He is also a rawhide braider. Because of his perfect smile, curly black lashes, and neatly creased hats, he has often been the subject of photos in calendars and magazines. And he enjoys the notoriety.

Nicknamed Scooter, he's bright, friendly, and steady. He has a talent with horses and rawhide as well as a fine sense of humor. His room in the bunkhouse is decorated with a calendar that stars himself and dozens of brightly colored wildrags and cowboy hats varying from black to silverbelly.

During a rare slow time one recent winter, the ranch manager asked him and another buckaroo to paint the bunkhouse. "Ed Bacon and I kinda just made it a little bit creative," Tim laughs, showing off the delicate hues of pink and blue.

The living room has a TV set, a couple of chairs, and an old couch. There's also Tim's Osborne splitter, which can make rawhide strings really thin and round.

"A lot of time, if you get rawhide too thick, it will bend in the middle and turn up on the edges," Tim says. "You can do everything on that machine. Ed's father made another machine that helps us, and I made a string cutter from scrap parts."

If the blades aren't sharp, cutting will fuzz up the dry part of the rawhide. Tim uses an awl for braiding, to go underneath the strings and tie the knots. He uses pliers, cutters, and a beveler or edger that helps the hide stay flat. He used to practice with scrap hide, tying buttons and making stampede strings.

Sometimes he hitches horsehair. Occasionally he uses colored nylon fishing line to hitch strings. "It's prettier, you know," he says. "They make

horsehair-hitched belts in prisons, and they use a lot of nylon line and call it horsehair. It's easier to learn to hitch fishing line."

Standard cost for a set of McGinnis reins is $250, including a romal, which represents about forty hours of work. Tim often braids while he's watching TV at night in winter, tying knots, trying to earn a little extra while enjoying a hobby. A few years back he made an extra fine set of reins from the hide of a black and white cow.

"The strings are really small," he explains, "and these reins would have to be for somebody who was showing horses. If they were used for working, they would probably get torn up because they are not real strong. If I can't get $650 for them I would rather give them away than sell them cheap. They are a pretty set of reins."

Sometimes he uses leather, which is tanned rawhide, but he prefers curing his own hides. He uses a lot of soap, Ivory preferred, so the hide will pull down tighter and stretch slightly. "When rawhide's dry, it can break if you pull too much," he says. One of his favorite skins came from a sick cow, about fifteen years old. She died in the truck on the way to slaughter and Tim dragged her off. He skinned her that night and took the hide and stretched it, keeping it damp in a moist sack until he was ready to cut the strings.

But Tim has more to do than skin cows and braid rawhide. He's assistant cow boss (or jigger boss) for the Twenty-Five Ranch, which runs cattle for seventy miles north of Battle Mountain. The ranch has a crew of ten in summer, a few less in winter. Generators run constantly from a power plant not far from the bunkhouse. Occasionally the buckaroos go to town, either to Battle Mountain, a couple of dozen miles away, or to Elko, which takes an hour longer.

"I like to go out and dance," Tim smiles. "I like to be with everybody, but I quit drinking 'cause it changes attitude and it ain't worth doing."

Tim was eighteen when he gave up alcohol and was working at a ranch in his home state of South Dakota. His mother and aunt were trick riders, and his grandfather was a stock contractor for the rodeo. Tim spent summers breaking colts, haying, and fencing. When his boss died, the rancher's wife replaced Tim with a couple to run the place. So, Tim set out for Wyoming with his friend Ed Bacon.

The young cowboys rounded up horses for the BLM until they saw an ad for the IL Ranch in Tuscarora, Nevada. Ed got a job as a ranch hand, and Tim started breaking colts. At the time, there were almost a dozen buckaroos on the crew tending twenty-five hundred mother cows besides calves, bulls, and horses. There they met Martin Black, Dean Tobias, and Bill Black, all mecate

makers and rawhiders who showed the South Dakota cowboys how to prepare hide and braid. Tim also credits Martin Black for teaching him a lot about horsemanship.

It wasn't long before Tim got promoted. The ranch manager considered him more responsible than the others, even though he was in his mid-twenties and the second youngest there. At times the IL crew would take two eight-horse teams hitched to wagons and would spend a month on the desert rounding up cows.

"I can only stand not having a shower up to a point," Tim says. "When we got to the last camp we all jumped in the stock tank and took a bath. At least we could clean off some of the old stuff!"

He moved on to the Winecup and Gamble ranches and later to the TS. Then he moved to the Twenty-Five, an old, established outfit with lots of mature trees, corrals, arenas, and outbuildings. The ranch has several trailers for married workers, a red and white ranch house, and the peacock-protected bunkhouse. It is surrounded by low, brush-covered hills.

At times young wanna-be cowboys show up at a ranch. "They offer to help, don't even get paid," Tim says. "They work for free, to learn, to get experience." But even when they start to earn their way, it doesn't get easier. The life can be lonely, and it's tough on women. "Cowboys can't fall in love with the wrong person because it's hard to live the way we do," Tim says. "I've lived all winter in a teepee, you know, and it was good for me but would have been hard on a girl."

When buckaroos are together on the desert, at a ranch rodeo or in a buckaroo saloon, they sometimes recite verse to one another. At the Big Loop Rodeo in Jordan Valley, Oregon, a few years back, a bunch of cowboys had built a campfire and were making coffee. "It was cold that morning," Tim recalls, "and Waddie Mitchell—he looks like a plain old buckaroo—gets up and starts saying a poem just like it was a conversation."

Tim says Larry Schutte is another good reciter who might casually ask if the cowboys remember old Joe or the tale of a certain horse. "It's really amazing what he can do. Larry's style is different. He's got his own little technique. He stands like a rod and can just say poem after poem."

Tim knows the cowboy life can be punishing, that there are easier ways to earn a living, but he says he's not much interested in money. "Maybe someday I will be, but right now I've got the happiest job in the world. To me this isn't a job, it's fun, because I can be free out here. I work as long as it takes to get my chores done. I rope a lot, ride my horses, and I love to braid. If you are a doctor or lawyer, you've got set patterns, and you can't get out of the patterns."

Working seven days a week, for two or three weeks in a row, he gets up about 5:30 in winter, an hour or two earlier in summer. He rides four or five hours, then rests his horse. "We might brand a few calves and let the cattle sit awhile, to mother them up. I can't say that we're workaholics because we're not. We learn how to make a job easy, and it's the same with riding. You learn first the right way, and you're going to make yourself better the longer you work at it. Some people think us cowboys are phony and think we don't work, but it's not so much the work—it's talent and knowledge and the ability to use every part of your body."

Occasionally someone will kid him about being a cowboy. "But being a cowboy is everything," he says. "I look at 'em and say, 'I'll bet you hate your job.' And they do. They sit in a tractor or in a big mining truck and they hate to go to work. I love being jigger boss. I love the roping. I work with a crew of good guys, and there's never been a time when a cowboy's been fired for being lazy. Every one of them gets up in the morning and goes and rides the circles checking the cattle."

Tim has taught Larry Schutte's son John to trick rope. They can sit for hours, just messing with a lariat. "Cowboys grow up with the lifestyle," he says. "You grow up with a hat on your head and I got eight more in my room."

When Tim McGinnis finds the time, he practices and improves his rawhiding. "It takes time, a good hide, and the knowledge you've gained from learning little tricks, like tying different knots," he says. "I make almost all my own stuff. I make my own chaps. Everything I do, I try to make it myself. Not because it's cheaper—it's just because it's yours."

Tim looks out from under his stingy-brim and hollers at a peacock that is strutting too close to his stretching rawhide. "You know," he says with a grin, "I'm not near as good as I'm gonna be."

YOU CAN'T FOOL A KID

I came down from the mountains, and gave this lad a ride,
I pulled him up behind me, his unbelieving eyes were wide.

He said, "You look to be a cowboy, but are you really one?
I see the hat and saddle, and the rope and saddle gun."

"I see the pointy boots and pistol, and old worn out blue jeans,
And your legs are bowed a little, not straight by any means."

"I see the big belt buckle, and Bull Durham in your shirt,
And your horse and you and all your gear, are covered up with dirt."

"And your eyes are squinty, and your face is really tanned,
You swear a lot and need a shave, your horse has a rancher's brand."

"But you can't really be for sure, what you pretend you are,
If you really are a cowboy, sir, then show me your guitar."

Carl "Skinny" Rowland

JOHN WEINKAUF The Boot Maker

Catering to connoisseurs, this Nevada craftsman makes boots for people

who demand perfection.

Weinkauf's interpretation of the traditional butterfly design with inside pulls. The craftsman used white calfskin piping and kidskin in lime green, pink, purple, teal, and yellow. Vamp is full-quill lavender ostrich. Each piece of Weinkauf's boots is hand cut with a knife.

John Weinkauf always wears boots worthy of notice, and he often hears people say, "Those sure are nice looking, but you just can't get good boots anymore." A few custom boot makers like John, who lives in Washoe Valley, Nevada, are proving those folks wrong. These boot makers offer comfort and pure art, items pleasing to the eye, with curves, color, and style. One of John's buyers was so pleased with his boots that he now displays them on his living room mantle.

Another happy owner of John Weinkauf boots is Gordon Wilson, a former saddle maker and cowboy who is now a dentist in Tucson, Arizona. "I hate sneakers," Wilson says, "and it gets deep around here."

Wilson has already bought twenty pairs of Weinkauf boots. He wears a triple-A size fourteen. He likes high heels and a variety of color and skin. "I've tried a lot of boot makers, but some of their boots were crude and they hurt my feet," the dentist says. "Boots made by John Weinkauf fit. The rest don't."

John modestly says Wilson had a special problem, a painful spot on the ball of his foot. So John changed the way he made Wilson's boots. He built the bottom up with a thick insole and molded it, adding an indentation to disperse the pressure.

"All I could do was try to help him," John says. "It worked."

John, born in 1951, grew up on a small ranch outside Tucson, Arizona. He always liked leather and often created things for his friends. Before he left school, he was making fringed clothing, handbags, luggage, and sandals for a merchant in town. It wasn't long before he became a partner in the shop.

"We mostly made zillions of sandals, but when we started selling Lucchese boots I was totally amazed at the quality work they were doing," he says. "It excited me. It made me feel really good that somebody could do something that fine, because there's not many people who can make boots."

He started to follow the Luccheses' lead, accumulating "lasts," which are the forms used to build boots. "I started using American Standard lasts, which are just about what everybody uses, with the exception of makers of custom boots or special-order boots. I would measure the feet and correlate those to the last, and modify them. Some people have a wide ball of the foot, a high instep, or a low instep. There are lots of variations."

The last determines height of the heel. If the heel is the proper height, the

boots will stand perpendicular to the ground, not lean backward or forward. The wearer should be able to rock on the front of the boot a little bit.

After a few years, John split with his partner. He moved his equipment into his garage and slowly acquired more machines and tools.

"I just wanted to be a boot maker," he says. "I've been working at it ever since."

John and his wife Becky moved to Nevada in 1983 with their three chil-

dren. He built a large shop next to their house, which is one of the oldest in Washoe Valley, north of Carson City. He added more equipment to help his craft. His favorite is a fifty-year-old sewing machine that he uses for top stitching. "It works great," John says. "I've sewn on brand-new machines that don't sew as good as that."

For two decades, John has been making boots for people everywhere—from New York to Florida, Texas to California, Canada to Australia. His reputation has spread through magazine stories, word of mouth, and shows. He constantly experiments with colors, skins, and styles, gaining a liking for ostrich, anteater, alligator, elephant, buffalo, kangaroo, and waxed calf.

He makes cowboy boots in several styles—laceups and pull-ons, short (peewee) boots, and tall (riding) boots. He buys leather in the best grades and makes sure the colors are impregnated properly into the hides. "Generally when you find a painted skin, it's an inferior grade that has scars, warble holes, bug bites," he says.

One hunter brought him the skin from an elephant. John made him five pairs of boots, three briefcases, and a few belts. "There's approximately one thousand square feet of skin on an elephant. It was so massive it was cut into pieces, each the size of a sheepskin."

John's pull-on base price is $400. He charges more for anything over a twelve-inch top and for exotic skins, additional stitching, overlays, brands, inlays, or special collars. "It's time and effort," he says. "Most of the fancy pull-ons cost about $650."

He works in his shop seven days a week, at times from daylight to midnight. He has a waiting list of about six months, sometimes longer if he's searching for an exotic or special grade of skin.

Caring for boots is as important as making them, John says. Leather is like human skin, basically pure protein, and needs attention. He says anything you can put on your skin you can put on leather. Some of his customers use Noxzema on their boots.

"Creams help boots hold up real well," he says, "especially for things like lizard, which will bust on you because of the flex joints in the skin." Commercial cleaners may contain turpentine, acetone, or other chemicals that are bad for leather even though they'll produce a good shine. John says, "If you have

Close-up of fancy woman's boot. Weinkauf carries his attention to detail even into color combinations for the stitching.

boots made of a very fine calfskin, you don't want to put heavy grease on the leather because they're not compatible."

He recommends polishes like Tanner and Meltonian, which are more like a cream than a heavy wax. (Avoid polishing on top of dirt; it's abrasive.) Cornhuskers' lotion works on many skins. Saddle soap is good for washing boots. "It works like soap on your skin. After you wash with it, then add polish or cream."

The difference between a really fine boot and a cheaply made boot is found in the time that goes into it, the detail, and the leather's quality. Calfskin can range from $3 a foot to $8 a foot. Some cattle will have cuts or too many brands. Grading depends on the quality of the animal. "You can only do so much with one set of hands," John says. "I use the best materials possible even though I've got a very limited market."

Every boot buyer has his or her quirks, John says. "You need to know what kind of socks they like to wear, thick or thin. You need to know if they are more comfortable with a looser boot, or if they have problems with their feet."

When he analyzes a client's feet, he makes notes in a scrapbook, lists materials and measurements. He traces each foot and measures the ball, the low instep, the high instep, and then the high instep to the base of the heel. Once the customer decides what he or she wants, John sits down with the skins, lays out his patterns, and goes to work.

"Every foot is unique," he says. "There are some designs that you don't want to use on some people's feet because they are harder to get into."

He enjoys working with strong colors like bougainvillea, turquoise, red, and powder blue. He has worked his patterns out over time. During his boot-making career, he's gone through four different sets of patterns. Every time he makes a new one, he changes the style, the sizing, or the tightness of the throat. "They are all integral parts of how it fits together so that when you pull it on the form, it fits properly."

He first cuts the vamp, the part that needs the best material. "You cut the leather according to the stretch, which has to go from toe to heel. If you cut it going across the ball of the foot, the boot will bag out after a while. Factory boot makers don't care how they cut their leather." After the vamp, he cuts the foxing, at the back of the boot. Then he'll cut the linings and the tops.

All cutting is done first, including vamp, foxing, collar, pull straps (also called pulls or mule ears), special piping, or inlays. Linings are glued in and then sewn.

"Your first line of stitching is the most important because it's the foundation for the rest. If your first line is crooked, every line after that is going to be off at the same spot."

He sews a line of gray, followed by a line of pink, then burgundy and bougainvillea. He has put as many as eight rows on a boot. "Some people want more than that, but four or five seem to look best."

The lining leather is tanned so it can flex and hold up against perspiration. It's soft, supple, but not so stretchy that it's going to lose its shape. When a

These lace-up boots, known as packers, have teal goatskin tops with brown waxed-calf vamp and foxing, stitched toe wrinkle, and welted sole. Waxed calf is actually rough-out with the nap waxed down to give a glazed effect. The advantage of waxed calf is that it's strong and doesn't scuff or scratch. In the old days waxed calf came only in black, and resin from inside stoves was used to wax boots. Now the leather is available in several colors.

*Peewee boot, 1940s
style, square toe.
Vamp is roughout,
with mink-colored
ostrich plug inset.
Top is metallic
brush-off goat skin.
Inside pull tabs,
star perforations
around the collar,
and inlaid five-point
star on front.*

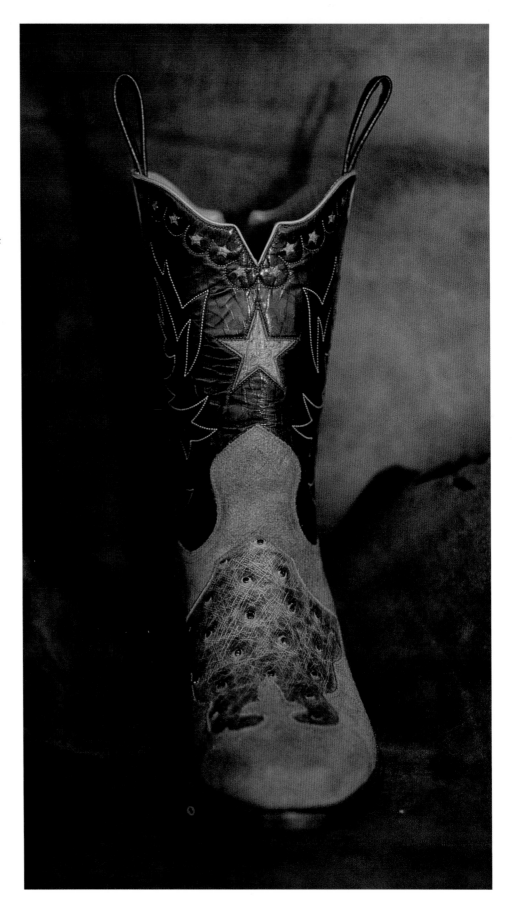

really big guy requests an ostrich boot, which is a soft skin, John puts in a double lining so it won't distort. "Heavy guys are tough on boots," he laughs.

Scissors and knives trim and cut boots. The handle of a hammer smoothes the seams. The side welt, or seam, helps visually and also strengthens a boot. It is at a strategic spot so it has to be sewn tightly because it gets a tremendous amount of stretching and pressure when the boot is pulled onto the foot.

On low-cost boots, plastic sidewalls are used, which shrink and swell and leave a rough edge. On John's boots, if he's making them for a working cowboy who likes oxbow stirrups, he'll use a sixty-penny nail between the insole and outsole instead of a spring steel shank. He beats the front and back flat, bends it to the shape of the arch, then sews it in by hand.

The welt connects the uppers to the sole, which is the final piece John assembles. The sole varies in thickness depending on the size of the person and size of the boot. After John sews on the soles, he trims the edges and pegs the shank. "The welting only goes around the vamp," John explains. "I do it that way because you get a lot more of a contour in fit in the arch, more comfort, and you get a cleaner look."

When he's working hard, John can make two pairs of boots a week, averaging twenty-five to thirty hours a pair. "There's two hundred and forty-some-odd steps in making a pair of boots, and each step, if it's done right, fits together right."

Boot making is a difficult profession, because boots get a lot of hard use and because feet (and customers' egos) can be sensitive. John says, "A cowboy will moan if boots bug him." John Weinkauf guarantees that his will be comfortable. They are trimmed down delicately. They are refined. Their detailed finish work, John says, is "something nobody else wants to do generally. It is something that takes a lot of time and a lot of pride."

Boots weren't always so stylish. Until the late 1800s, John says, there were no lefts and rights. Cosimo Lucchese, who came from Italy in 1886 and set up his famous boot shop in San Antonio, primarily made cavalry boots. He introduced machinery and used a steam-powered inseaming machine. He was one of the first people to develop lasts and standardize sizes.

"It was a very new era," John says. "He and his son Sam were master boot makers. They did some fantastic work."

During Cosimo Lucchese's time, there were a dozen boot makers on the same street close to his original shop. When one craftsman closed for the day, others came and looked in the window to check out the merchandise. "Pretty soon they'd be shuffling ideas and it became very competitive. The good ones just got better."

John points out that Lucchese Boot Company had such a good reputation that in the 1940s Acme Boot Company hired the Italians to make boots depicting the states. Each pair took at least two hundred hours to make, and they subsequently have been displayed in stores and museums across the country.

"Windows for the capitol buildings are even cut out and sewn in," John says. "The state bird and flower is on each boot. They have never been worn. They have been taken on tour, displayed in Denver and San Antonio, and there's some at the Lucchese factory. Lucchese made beautiful stuff."

Besides beautiful boots, John himself also makes fancy purses, belts, chaps, chinks, notebook covers, and briefcases. Everything is in leather. His custom boots are always one-of-a-kind, guaranteed to fit and be of good quality.

"I can make boots for most people," John says. "But maybe a guy has high blood pressure or he's used to wearing real baggy clothes and he likes to kick his boots off when he gets home. Well, he doesn't want a fitted boot. He's wasting his money unless he wants a particular color or skin or he wants a brand sewn on the tops."

One fellow who went to see John a few years back said he'd had boots made by everyone including Lucchese. He wanted a pair that really fit. John asked him how snug he liked them, so the man went out to his truck and brought in a pair of boots.

"He was an older gentleman, probably seventy," John recalls. "He gets these boots and tries to get them on, and his foot got about four inches below the top of the boot. Then they got tight. He turned every color of red that you can imagine and finally had to slam his foot into the boot. When he stood up, he got dizzy and said, 'That's how I want them to fit.'"

John smiled and said, "OK, now I know."

Nathan throws a loop as several horses anticipate the catch.

ARE YOU A COWBOY?

When they ask, "Are you a cowboy?"
I kinda consider the source . . .
Is it someone who thinks I'm flush
And's tryin' to sell me a horse?

Or a downtown type in tennis shoes
Who's skeptical but courteous
And never smelled one of our kind
Up close, and's only curious.

The first guy really wants to know
Are you any good around stock?
Can you help a calvy heifer,
Can you dally and double hock?

You know how to use a bosal?
Can you mouth 'em and read a brand?
He never says it straight out loud
But he's askin', "Are you a hand?"

The other guy, who's just as nice,
Don't know a tit from a wattle!
And when he asks, "Are you for real?"
I quote the Greek, Aristotle,

Who might have answered had he lived
"Son, don't count on bein' lucky . . .
To find out if he lives with cows
Examine his boots for pucky!"

I like to think I'm good with cows,
A pretty fair hand with a horse.
But am I a sure fire cowboy?
I'm dodgin' the answer, of course.

I've learned to handle the question
Whichever one wants to know it.
I ante up and say that I'm
A better cowboy poet!

Baxter Black

TONI SCHUTTE Fine Art on the Range

During long, cold winters this Nevada cowgirl creates buckaroo art.

Diamond-pattern hitched-hair belts by Toni Schutte. Time involved is about one inch of hitching per hour.

Some women crochet. Toni Schutte hitches hair into horse jewelry. She does ink sketches of equines, cattle, and kids. She cooks, cleans, and helps husband Larry make mecates. She encourages son John with his 4-H stock and daughter Reata when she plays her fiddle. But this petite and beautiful dark-eyed woman of Portuguese descent can also rope and ride as well as most buckaroos.

Her family had a feed lot in California and moved to Nevada and bought a ranch when she was six months old. She married Idaho cowboy Larry Schutte (pronounced Shooty) in the mid-seventies and moved around the Great Basin from ranch to ranch as Larry improved his lot from buckaroo to cow boss to ranch manager. Today they live on the Quarter Circle S Ranch near Tuscarora, Nevada. Toni and Larry have many friends amongst the wandering cowboys. One of them, Bill Black, introduced Toni to hitching horsehair.

"He was living down in Dixie Valley and had bought a piece of hitched-hair work at a pawn shop. He had taken it apart to see how it was made," she says. "He told me all you needed to know was how to half hitch and count horse tail hairs."

She thought about it for years but wouldn't try it. When she finally did attempt it, she created a heck of a mess and gave it up. But the quitting wasn't permanent. Two years later, another of Toni's friends made a beautiful quirt. "It was the first one he'd done, and he showed me how easy it really was."

She experimented, twisting binder twine to learn how ropes were put together. She used rawhide, mohair, anything to see if it would stay together. "You could twist up stripped sheets if you wanted to—it would make a rope."

Finding hair is not a problem for Toni. The mane hair Larry uses for mecates always comes mixed with tail hair. Tail hair is too coarse for Larry's ropes but perfect for hitching because of the length. Toni sorts through it and pulls out the long hairs, some of which can be up to three feet.

When she began, Toni was teaching herself. Trial and error, error and trial. She wanted to learn more, but there was no one around who could show her how to make bosals and quirts, belts and hat bands. She eventually found an Australian book that explained the middle stages. "They didn't show you how to get started. They didn't show how to finish. They just said, 'Take the string and . . .'"

She laughs. It took her a long time to figure out the typical hitched-hair diamond pattern. The one she copied from the book was called the Bushman. "If I want a stripe, I hitch one row one way, and, when I come back around, I hitch the whole row the other way. That will give you a straight stripe."

The base of the work is leather, or rawhide, or even wire if a buyer wants a stiff piece of work. Toni will practice on anything, and as a result there are plenty of pens, pencils, and bottles covered with hitched hair at the ranch "just for decoration." She says her early pieces were rough, but Larry disagrees.

Toni Schutte draws in pen and ink, and hitches hair. Her husband Larry makes ropes, daughter Reata plays fiddle, son John paints and does trick roping. The whole family helps Larry twist mecates.

"Her first hitched-hair nosepiece on a bosal was a pretty booger," he claims. With the money she earned from it, she bought a vacuum cleaner.

She received a grant from the Nevada State Council on the Arts to be taught by Wyoming master hitcher Doug Krause. Her work improved rapidly. Because of Krause, she saw many other artists' work, which further inspired her. She noticed that much of the work from Mexico has long hitches, up to a quarter-inch, whereas most Great Basin hitches are tiny—little more than the width of the string or about five tail hairs.

One of Toni's problems was that she didn't pull as tight one way as she did the other, so one side had more twist and wasn't perfectly smooth. Although she found it difficult to match the ends of a piece of work, she saw others had the same problem. "Some guys use a button to cover it up because they can't get it to match." Her early work included key chains and buttons on horsehair tassels, which she gave away. The rings on tassels are either rawhide, which looks better, or metal, which makes more sense.

"A metal ring won't break," she says. "Usually cowboys put them on their cinch for decoration, and when they're riding through the brush, a piece of sagebrush can jerk the rawhide ones off." Lately she has been making bosal nose buttons, barrettes, and fancy, hitched-hair belts. She hitched a miniature quirt for Larry to use as a key chain.

Faith is important to Toni and her family, who belong to Cowboys for Christ. Larry preaches sometimes and plays music at prayer meetings. "To belong, it doesn't mean you got to be a cowboy, and it don't matter what church you go to," the Catholic-raised Toni says.

She claims her work is for the Lord, but the labor is obviously all hers. Hair hitching requires patience and desire, not to mention a good quantity of usable horsehair. "Tail hair is sturdier than mane hair, and that's what you want. I have a long board with tape on it. I count hairs, about five at a time, and then tie them in a knot. That's what I half-hitch, one stitch at a time. Sometimes white hair is really thin so it takes a few more light hairs than it does dark hair—maybe five black to seven white—to keep the work even."

Toni's first bosal brought in enough money for a new vacuum. "I cleaned up with that bosal," she laughs.

**Hitched-hair bosal
and decorative
throatlatch tassel.**

Her patterns include diamonds, zigzags, stripes, and spirals. "To make a diamond is very difficult," Toni says. She leans over her work, carefully counting hairs. She uses waxed thread as a base, the same material used for sewing boots and saddles. "Start with a knot, a row of knots, then start hitching each one. That's all it is."

When the hair runs out, she has to splice new ones in. "You can bury a hair underneath, next to the base, and pull a new one in." One great hitcher's work impressed Toni. "It was really smooth because he buried the whole string underneath and brought a new one up. Wow! That was a lot easier than the way I was doing it!"

Toni's first bosal took a very long time. She used to wax the hairs after she'd counted them so they'd stay together. "When you're hitching, you have

Toni practices hitching on anything that's handy. Most of her pens are decorated.

to recount them, and I was really getting frustrated. A guy named Steve, who's really good, just said, "Tie a knot in the end of them.' I thought, 'Oh yeah?' But it works!"

There have been years at the Elko County Fair when Larry has competed in the branding and he and John have shown winning reining and cutting horses, when Reata has earned blue ribbons for her lambs and calves and for baking, and Toni has won the team penning as well as ribbons for her art.

Toni Schutte and her family will continue to rope, ride, tend cattle, play music, and sing. They enjoy working hard and thanking the Lord often for being together. Elko is about seventy miles away, and the only improvement Toni could think of would be to live further from town.

"I like things quiet," she says. "I like the pace slow."

A COWBOY'S PRAYER

Oh Lord, I've never lived where churches grow.
    I love creation better as it stood
That day You finished it so long ago
    And looked upon Your work and called it good.
I know that others find You in the light
    That's sifted down through tinted window panes,
And yet I seem to feel You near tonight
    In this dim, quiet starlight on the plains.

I thank You, Lord, that I am placed so well,
    That You have made my freedom so complete;
That I'm no slave of whistle, clock or bell,
    Nor weak-eyed prisoner of wall and street.
Just let me live my life as I've begun
    And give me work that's open to the sky;
Make me a pardner of the wind and sun,
    And I won't ask a life that's soft or high.

Let me be easy on the man that's down;
    Let me be square and generous with all.
I'm careless sometimes, Lord, when I'm in town,
    But never let 'em say I'm mean or small!
Make me as big and open as the plains,
    As honest as the hoss between my knees,
Clean as the wind that blows behind the rains,
    Free as the hawk that circles down the breeze!

Forgive me, Lord, if sometimes I forget.
    You know about the reasons that are hid.
You understand the things that gall and fret;
    You know me better than my mother did.
Just keep an eye on all that's done and said,
    And right me, sometimes, when I turn aside,
And guide me on the long, dim, trail ahead
    That stretches upward toward the Great Divide.

Badger Clark

BILL HELM Bits of Heavy Metal

After working for years with rust and iron, this Fallon craftsman

switched to copper, silver, and shiny cold-rolled steel.

Style of cold-rolled bit, with overlaid silver concho.

"My dad was not much of a dairyman," says Bill Helm, sitting in the shade of a leafy cottonwood outside his place at the edge of Fallon, Nevada, near the Forty Mile Desert. "We had a dairy in the San Joaquin Valley, but my dad sold it and bought a cattle ranch near Doyle, California, in 1948."

He was thinking of his father, John Helm, who was a rancher, horse trader, saddle bronc rider. He was thinking of his uncle, Cliff Helm, who was a world

Bill Helm, son of a rancher, worked as an ironworker until he was injured. Then he became a maker of bits and spurs and, still a cowboy at heart, keeps a few cows.

champion cowboy in the twenties. And he was thinking of the ranch at Doyle, north of Reno, that became his new home when he was a kid.

To get a teacher assigned to the ranch, there had to be four children of school age. "But there were only three," Bill recalls, "so Larry Dickinson's family brought a cousin to live on the ranch. We got a teacher, and she lived at the schoolhouse."

Bill was breaking horses before his teens but he seldom got to a rodeo because his family simply didn't have the time. "You rode, you checked pumps, fixed fence, fed hay, did chores. There was not much entertainment time."

When he was thirteen, his parents divorced, and Bill moved to town with his mother and sister. He attended Reno High School, but he says he learned a whole lot better out at the ranch. At seventeen he joined the Navy and spent four years in the service, later regretting that he did not stay longer. He spent his last few weeks in Vietnam, "but it was just starting when I was getting out."

Back in Reno, he got a job driving a truck, hauling dirt. He met Gayle and married her. Then he bartended for a while until his father called him for help. John Helm had big plans, as usual, and was not content staying in one place with a single purpose. He had married again and bought a ranch fifty miles south of Ely in Lincoln County. So Bill quit his job, and he and Gayle packed a stock truck with all their belongings and moved east. On their way to the ranch, Gayle kept asking, "When are we going to get there? When are we going to get there?" and Bill would reply, "Just over that mountain." But they'd keep going over mountains, one after the other, and for hours there was no end in sight. Finally they arrived.

"Gayle had never been out of the city limits of Reno," Bill says. "She wasn't a ranch girl. In eastern Nevada we had no power, just oil lamps or Coleman lanterns. The washing machine had a gasoline motor. She just about had a fit."

The ranch had a few cattle, and they ran a little rodeo, furnishing bucking stock. "But it was one of them normal relation deals," Bill says. "No money, no this, no that."

John got haying contracts, and sent Bill and his stepbrother to do all the work. "My father had a wonderful gift of gab, but he was always looking over the hill to greener pastures. He was always off with the new venture." One day John Helm went to town to the bank to borrow money to buy cattle. But he didn't buy cattle. He bought a motel instead and moved it to the ranch, planning to turn it into a hunting lodge.

"He was going to make a killing," recalls Gayle, who never saw any money for their work. She remembers feeling trapped because they had no car, no cash, and very peculiar prospects. "We had stayed all summer, and all I wanted was out of there," she says. "My mother came to get me, and we all moved back."

Bits and spurs,
showing Bill Helm's
ingenuity.

Bill got a job with Reno Iron Works in 1963. He was already a welder and a blacksmith. "My dad was an ironworker, too, off and on—he built horseshoes." Bill worked on high rises as an independent contractor, earning a better paycheck than he would have received working for his father or as a buckaroo. The family, now with three kids, lived south of Reno in Washoe Valley and had a few horses. Then they moved to the outskirts of Fallon in 1978.

"Washoe Valley was too crowded," Bill complains. "Every time I wanted to ride a colt, kids on motorcycles would be zooming by. That was hell."

Also, Bill had been injured several times on the job. While working on a crew strengthening the state capitol building in 1978 to make it earthquake-proof, he fell off a crane. "That was the third time I broke my back." He took a medical retirement and was retrained by the state as a bit and spur maker.

"I could have made them," he says, "but there was a lot of stuff I didn't know. I learned a lot working with a bit maker named Kirk Robot." With Robot's help, Bill learned quickly.

Bits and spurs by Bill Helm are made by hand, one at a time. He has no machinery and only a few jigs. "You make an iron pattern, a jig, so that each piece you make is identical. If you tried to make twenty cheek pieces or mouthpieces on the anvil, there'd be quite a difference between them, and it would take you twice as long to do it." His prices are in the middle range: cheaper than the fancy inlaid silver work, higher than manufactured bits from Korea and Taiwan.

"I've been a working person all my life. I've traded horses. I had all my kids in high school rodeos and know what it takes to buy this gear. I wanted to build handmade stuff with silver on it and everything else, but I wanted to keep the price down so it's something a working man can afford."

Bill Helm spurs cost about $150 to $200. His bits start at $100. He orders plain silver conchos from Diablo in California, then adds design. He engraves and overlays the silver, hand cuts the sterling silver initials, numbers, and bars, and also twists the silver rope edging. He uses jeweler's bronze instead of gold. "It's harder and doesn't wear as much, and you can't tell the difference."

He makes spurs for bull riders, bronc riders, cutting horse riders, and buckaroos. "Cutting horse riders like a real long shank. They are not supposed to move their feet. If they spur, they don't want the judges to see them do it." Buckaroo spurs generally have chap guards and large rowels. Ropers' spurs have a dull, small rowel. "They use their feet a lot and really jab the horse. They want something dull so that they can be serious yet not hurt the horse."

Advertising nothing, he has reps selling his merchandise in California, Oregon, Montana, Idaho, and Nevada. He gets custom orders direct from the D-Bar-M Western Store in Reno and relies on word of mouth. Since he went into the bit and spur business, he's always had orders.

He prefers making spurs. "Bits are harder, but you get less money for them." Some bits from custom makers have parts manufactured abroad. "The mouthpieces and cheeks are often made in Korea and then assembled here," he says. "Some mouthpieces in custom bits are made by machine. Mine aren't. My mouthpieces, I have to heat and beat."

In Bill Helm's workshop, where he has hung photos of his father and uncle

and of his kids at high school rodeos, there is metal everywhere. His supplies are basically flatbar, solid bars of varying widths. "I make everything out of cold-roll wire. I don't use any stainless. Everything is cold rolled, and then I temper it."

He believes cold-rolled steel is better because it has a sweet taste that horses seem to like. He doesn't believe stainless should be used for a bit or spurs. "They never had stainless steel back when they were really cowboying."

He uses a hammer and a torch, cutting and welding pieces of spur together, curving them exactly right. He has a forge outside the shop and a couple of anvils. After the silver is engraved and in place, he blues most of his work with a torch or gun-blueing because he likes the way it looks.

"Gun-blueing is a liquid—you paint it on. After a while it will wear off and will be like a fine rust." Oiling spurs keeps them nice, and he suggests that a little spray of oil will bring back the color.

Copper parts in the roller bits are made from copper wire, and Bill twists the soft metal with a small tool. "It entertains the horse." He makes copies of old U.S. cavalry bits. He makes special bits for reining people and cutting horse people. "I've got four different mouthpieces that I make and about eight standard bits." For rope edging, he uses silver wire and twists it, then solders it on. The conchos he buys are nickel and covered with a thin layer of silver.

Many people have sent Bill Helm drawings of the bits and spurs they want. Some want six points on a spur rowel, others may want twice as many. He helps them, but he doesn't want to make an item that doesn't make sense or could hurt the horse. "I can do anything you want, up to a point, but you're going to pay for it. If you want more silver, it's more money."

For many years, Bill Helm has donated a pair of spurs or a silver bit to the Pony Bob Rodeo in Reno. "It's good for those kids," he smiles. In the workshop in Fallon there's a picture of Bill on the cover of one of the Pony Bob's past programs. It says, "Bill Helm custom bits and spurs, hand crafted quality. We forge them to your fancy."

The cold-roll that Bill uses, often called sweet iron, will rust. "Dudes are the ones that want the shiny stuff. They are the ones that have a horse and an acre and go to town and buy a Sears and Roebuck saddle and a Korean bit. I think spurs look better and bits look better when they get rusty than when

Spurs made of cold-rolled steel, with overlaid silver, chap guards, and two-inch rowels.

they are blue. The rust shows off the silver. And it don't get the kinda rust like you think, big flakes of iron. It's a smooth rust when you're wearing them all the time. I think that's what a cowboy likes."

In summer Bill gets itchy. As a cure, he goes out contract haying. In winter he's happier. "When it's cold I don't mind it because I hurt so bad from broken bones I don't mind staying inside." He has never gone to his shop with nothing to do. He still is partial to cattle and runs a few for old-times' sake and for trading purposes. "I might need my truck overhauled," he laughs.

He looks over his small spread toward the sun setting over the desert and looks affectionately at a middle-aged gelding. "I call him Wimp. He was registered Wimpy Bar None, but I'm not one of them that go for all that registry. He just happened to have been that way. He's quite a pest, fourteen now, but what I like about him is you can do anything with him. You can pull anything, you can rope anything. He's so fat. He and I make a good pair."

HATS, BRITCHES, BOOTS, SPURS 'N CHAPS (excerpt)

The cowboy wore spurs on his boot heels,
And clanked 'em like musical bell peals,
     He kicked up so high,
     He caught his own thigh—
Now he knows how his suffering horse feels.

Gwen Petersen and Jeane Rhodes

SCOTT BROWN Man of the Saddle

To figure out how to make a saddle right, this Kansas country boy

became a buckaroo.

**Scott Brown's shop
is in an alley behind
his home in Elko.
He is holding his son
Eric.**

Scott Brown was a dreamer. He had always lived in Kansas. He had never been on a horse, never met a cowboy. He was a roofer, a carpenter, and worked awhile as a donut cook. He attended college for a few hours. "Nothing serious," he laughs. "I enjoyed college but didn't know what it could do for me."

What Scott Brown did know was that he liked leather.

He moved to Texas at the tender age of nineteen, married Becky, and signed up for a one-year saddle making class at a technical school in Amarillo. While attending school he made five saddles. After he graduated, he took one of them to Ryan's, a saddle shop in Fort Worth.

"I guess they were impressed with it," he says, "because they put me to work."

Ryan's sold hats, boots, western clothes, and tack. What made the store different was the fact that it had a saddle shop (much like Leddy Bros. a few blocks away, where Eddie Brooks got his start).

"I learned a lot at Ryan's," Scott says. "It was kinda fun 'cause you have several guys, and you're all trying to outdo each other, trying to get better."

The first week he earned $200 doing piecework. When Tandy Corporation bought out Ryan's eighteen months later, Scott was earning more money but didn't want to stay in a corporate atmosphere.

He had heard stories about Elko, Nevada, from a fellow student who had cowboyed in the Great Basin. He learned about J. M. Capriola's, a well-respected western store in Elko. He knew that Eddie Brooks, a master saddle maker originally from Fort Worth, was managing Capriola's saddle shop. Scott asked Eddie for a job and went to work.

"Eddie's a great guy, top-notch," Scott says. "He taught me a lot."

For three and a half years, Scott worked in a cubbyhole in the back of the upstairs shop. "They treated me good, but it got to be time to go. I still had never ridden or cowboyed, and I wanted to learn something about it. I'd been making the damn saddles for years but didn't know how to use them."

Bill Kane at the Spanish Ranch gave him a chance. Scott already had bought a horse and taught himself to ride. He didn't know much about roping, though.

The second day he was there, they had to rope out some calves during weaning. "I roped that first one," he laughs. "I told Bill Kane that was the first

Herman Oak Leather Company in St. Louis has been in the tanning business since the 1800s. Scott Brown and other great saddle makers get their cowhide from them because they offer the finest quality. Here Scott is "blocking one out," cutting the pieces extra large so he can hand trim each one for an exact fit. Factory-built saddles are "clicked out" on dies.

thing I'd ever roped, and he looked at me as if I was from Mars. He couldn't believe it." But many of the Great Basin ranches are the same. "If you've got try, if you want to learn, they'll help you."

Scott says it doesn't take much to pick up the basics of cowboy work. It's not hard to fit in, to get along with the crew, to earn your wages. "If you're keeping your eyes open and your mouth shut and trying to learn something, it doesn't take too long. But to get good—now you're talking years!"

The Spanish Ranch paid Scott $550 a month. "That may sound good for a single guy, but for a married guy it wasn't, with no free beef and no insurance, and then Becky got pregnant while we were there." When another job came up at Maggie Creek, he took it. It paid better, $800 a month plus beef and insurance. He was one of two buckaroos at a camp called Red House, taking care of a thousand cows. When the other cowboy left, they gave Scott the camp. It was a good arrangement for Scott and Becky. "We were comfortable, and I was still making saddles on the side."

When he was at Capriola's Scott says he was shy about talking to guys because he didn't know anything about buckarooing. Perhaps because he was working cattle, he got a reputation, fast, as a good saddle maker. Orders started coming in. At Red House he did the majority of his saddle making in winter—during spring and fall he was too busy.

Scott and Becky's son Austin was born at Red House, but after a year out in the brush the family returned to Elko. They bought a small house in the Basque neighborhood close to the Star Hotel. The house, located in the old red-light district, had a tiny garage in back, and Scott turned it into a saddle shop.

"Becky was scared of me going out on my own. I had no insurance, no salary, no orders either. I had $900, my tools and my stock, and a couple of trees. I had people promise me orders, more or less. They'd say, 'Oh yeah, I'll order one.'"

Saddles are expensive, usually well over $1,000, and buckaroos don't earn much money. But if they want a new saddle, they find a way to get it, even if it means borrowing money from a rancher against future wages.

"That first winter was kinda lean," Scott says. "We came here in the fall, and I had to order trees [the saddles' wooden bases]. I ordered six and sat around here all that winter waiting for trees. When the guy finally sent them, he sent six at a time with a thousand-dollar bill, C.O.D. Why couldn't he just send one at a time so I could be doing something?"

He now uses trees by Todd McGiffin of Baker, Oregon. "I really like the way he builds his trees and the way the wood goes together in them. Todd's a perfectionist and always does me a good job."

Scott makes several styles of saddles. He gives Todd about eight different measurements, including style of the tree and shape and size of the horn. He often draws a picture, and Todd takes the time to meet Scott's specifications.

"That's pretty rare," Scott says. "A lot of tree makers won't do that. He uses fir for the most part. Other guys may use cottonwood and the factories use pine. You don't want to use a hardwood like oak because it's too heavy and too hard to work."

A tree known as the Wade tree, used in a slick-fork type saddle, is fairly common in the Great Basin. The clearance over the withers is adequate and the horn sits down closer to the horse, which helps when roping or working a horse. "The horn's out of the way. It's not sticking up in your face when you're roping, and the leverage is a lot closer to the horse so there's less strain on him." A swell fork, often called an Association tree, is more common elsewhere and is used by professional rodeo bronc riders.

Although 90 percent of good saddles work on most horses, Scott says, it's easier to fit horses than people. "For the 10 percent of the horses the saddle doesn't fit, you can use a cutout pad or make some adjustments for them." He often works for cowboys who travel, working different ranches. They don't want a saddle that fits one particular type of horse. "From one ranch to the next, the horses will change quite a bit. I adjust the seat length, the cantle width, things like that, to fit the man." Cowboys often have two saddles, one they ride most of the time and a second that's often, as Scott puts it, a "piece of junk they use for colts and stuff in case it gets busted up."

He says errors can be corrected on a saddle "if they're not too bad. Some of the guys, when I was learning, used to say a good saddle maker is not a guy that doesn't make mistakes—he's the guy that knows how to cover them up. Everyone's going to make mistakes. You learn to adjust and stretch it maybe a little more here or there so it doesn't stand out quite so bad."

Scott gets the hardware for his saddles from Pendleton, Oregon, including plates for the rigging. His leather comes from St. Louis, which he believes offers the best skirting leather.

Scott's base price of $1,200 for a slick or roughout includes no engraving or stamping. A slick uses the smooth side of the leather outside. A roughout's advantage is that it looks the same all the time; if it gets scratched up,

it doesn't hurt the appearance. "The drawback of a roughout is a lot of times they'll eat you; you stick to them and can't slide around. It's like Velcro." When they get older, however, they'll slick down.

Sometimes enjoying carving (hand-tooling and decorating the saddle), sometimes preferring to build roughouts, Scott goes through stages. He cuts one side of the seat, then folds the leather over and taps the two sides together so the design is indented on the second side and both sides can be cut exactly the same. It's the same with carving. "When I do the flower carving, I cut one side in and let it dry a little bit and then transfer it, or tap it over to the other side. Everybody has their own way of doing this kind of thing."

For the leather to form properly, it has to be damp. Scott likes to cut the pattern, wet it, and wrap it in a blanket overnight. "It gets the moisture real consistent through all the fibers of the leather. In the morning it's just a treasure to stamp."

Scott is fond of carving big flowers with gentle curves. "If you've got points, you can't get in underneath. I prefer big flowers because I can make them real nice."

If a buyer so desires, Scott will add silver, often ordering cheaper material from Mexico. "There are a few guys who will pay for Mark Dahl's silver inlay work," he says. "The weird thing is Mark's isn't that much higher and it's well worth the money."

He closed his shop in Elko a while back because he got a job at the Winecup Ranch. He's back to buckarooing full time, so he makes saddles when he has the time and the desire. Considering his dual work life, Scott's logo is appropriate—a saddle with tapaderos on it.

In winter, when the temperatures sink well below zero, Scott rides in a pair of bearskin chaps. "I made them myself and wear them for warmth," he says, "but they look classy, too." He uses bucking rolls on his own slick-fork saddle instead of a saddle with big swells. "It's just what you get used to," he says. "Bucking rolls are in a much more convenient position and are halfway soft, but a swell . . . that will beat you to death if you get in a fix."

High-quality slick-fork saddle with bucking rolls. This saddle has full flower stamp and is made on a Wade tree.

GO AND JUST BUCKAROO

They say with barbed wire came the fall of the West,
I ain't denyin' it's true.
'Cuz there's few places left, in this once empty West,
You can go and just buckaroo.

But you follow a fence and you'll find gate or hole,
And there you can wander on through.
But the days are gone, when you took horse and tack,
And could go and just buckaroo.

For the East runs this land, and they don't understand
About cows or our points of view.
They don't even care if they're playin' square,
Or care 'bout some lost buckaroo.

But throw the gate wide, 'cuz I'm still full of pride,
And I'll fight 'em till my life is through.
And out in the West, when they lay me to rest,
I'll go and just buckaroo.

Leon Flick

VICKIE SAILORS The Packer

When the dudes and hunters are away from her high mountain camp, this Montana woman hitches hair.

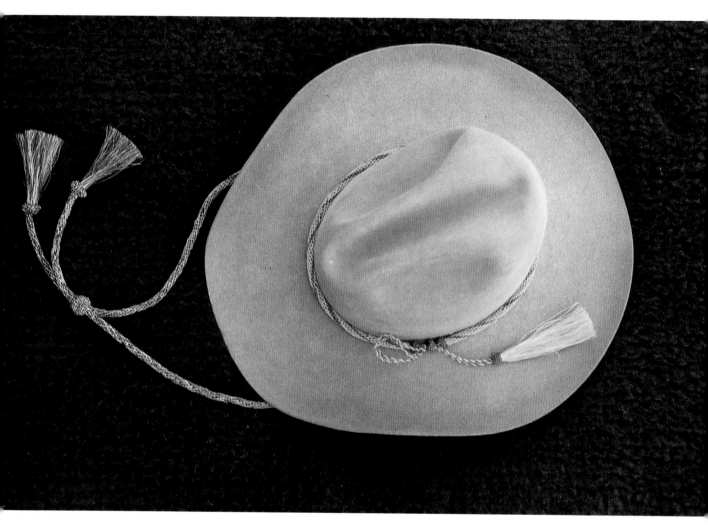

Hat with decorative hitched-hair band and stampede string (used to keep hat on in the wind and during a wild ride).

Vickie Sailors is blonde and strong with big blue eyes and a look that's clear and direct. She is barely forty and yet she and her brother Jeff have worked as packers for decades. She has managed a ranch. She has tended camps and cooked for hunters. And, in cowboy crafts, she has a knack for hitching hair.

"I like the old-time crafts," Vickie says. "I like making horse gear. I do a bit of braiding, but I always use hair, not rawhide."

The hair she uses is Mongolian pony hair, bought direct from China in two-pound bundles. "It comes really long, anywhere from twenty-eight to thirty-eight inches long, all one length, and it's really easy to work."

She has been hitching hair for three years, after learning the craft from Jeff, who has a reputation as a master hitcher. They both like to color (dye or bleach) their own horsehair. They add bright colors to already light hair and soak dark hair in peroxide to bleach the color out. "It gets blonde and comes out really neato," says Vickie. The shade depends on how long the dye or bleach is left on the hair.

"There's a lot of work involved other than actual hitching," she says. "There's pulling the hair, dying the hair, and then the hitching. Then you press it and do the knots on the ends, and those take a lot of time. And for belts, the leather has to be sewn on."

Most of her time is spent pulling, counting, and knotting the hairs. "First you get the hair, then pull out ten hairs and knot them together at one end—that's how you get what we call 'pulls.' Then you are ready to hitch."

All hitched-hair work comes out round, like a tube. A dowel is used as a base, sometimes made of rawhide, sometimes plastic. Vickie often wraps the base with twine, then half hitches over it, creating design by splicing in new colored hair.

Flat pieces such as belts and brow bands have to be pressed with a metal press. Vickie's press is made out of two pieces of half-inch channel iron measuring eight by forty inches. "You get the piece wet and press it for a couple of days. You can put it by a wood stove, and it'll dry in a day or two. Or put it outside in the sun."

She says if someone falls in a lake wearing a hitched-hair belt, it will swell up and have to be re-pressed. "But you could use two boards and do it yourself." Sometimes a hair will escape from a belt. "One guy thought it was like nylon. When a hair came loose, he took a lighted match to it and burned up the whole belt. People are insane!"

Vickie prefers making bridles and belts, but she also makes hat bands and stampede strings and does hitched-hair inlays in purses made of deer hide. Much of it is detail work. "You really have to be into doing little designs and thinking small."

Packer Vickie Sailors hitches hair while the dudes are away from her Rocky Mountain camp.

Before she got into the cowboy way, Vickie Sailors lived in Denver, where she worked as a bartender, delivered auto parts—"all sorts of stuff." She traveled and lived for a while in Wyoming and Utah. She's been in Montana fifteen years and admits to liking it best. "I've been cooking in Montana hunting camps and working for outfitters all this time." She prefers hunting camp because she always has spare time. "The hunters all leave and go looking for game, so I can hitch all day long."

A set of Vickie Sailors reins, including brow band and throat latch, costs about $600, although she points out, "There's more hitching on that than on a one-ear headstall, which costs $500." Hat bands run from $75 to $125, pocketbooks $100 and up, belts $250 and up. When either Vickie or Jeff gets a big order, they work together on it. "We don't compete," she says. "There's enough work for both of us."

Vickie Sailors enjoys working for outfitters and being alone in the high country. "Hitching takes a lot of time but you're always doing a different design," she says. "I particularly like it because it's nice to work for yourself."

Deer hide purses
with hitched-hair
handles and insets.

opposite:
All hair hitching is
done over a round
core. After the
work is complete,
purse handles are
ready but belts have
to be flattened in a
metal press.

Of course, she is working for a perfectionist: herself. Most people don't see the little errors that crop up in a piece, but Vickie does, and she says it drives her nuts. "I had to take out nine inches off a belt one summer—that's about nine hours' work. I always find a little flaw in what I do, even though other people say they see no problems. But I haven't made the perfect thing yet."

KINDRED SPIRITS

The spotted heifer missed the drive, and spent the winter, free,
Tho' "freedom's" price was willow bark, then sprigs of fillaree,
That, fin'ly, showed, beneath the snow, before her strength played out,
And "green-up" brought a fine bull calf, to teach the mav'rick route.

She fattened on the meadows, of the high Sierra's flanks,
In comp'ny of a mav'rick bull, that drifted from the ranks
Of cattle, 'cross the "Great Divide," turned loose, to make their way,
And lost amongst the canyons, that were strewn in disarray.

The offspring of the union, proved a wily beast, indeed,
Endowed with instincts from the wild, and blessed with wondrous speed,
That proved a worthy challenge, to punchers in the hills,
Who, thru the years, spun hairy tales, of wildest wrecks and spills.

But, tho' the issue, from the two, was sometimes trapped or caught,
These two ol' wily veterans, still practiced what they taught,
And spent each winter, runnin' free, within their secret haunt,
Which held enuff to see 'em thru, emergin' weak and gaunt.

For years, ol' "Utah" searched the range, in futile quest for sign,
Of where they spent the winter months, and somehow git a line,
On how they made it, ever' year, and brought a calf to boot,
Till fin'ly, one cold winter day, it fell to this ol' coot,
To happen on their winter park, hid out from pryin' eyes,
And to this day, ol' Utah holds the key to where it lies.

The kindred spirit, shared by all, who seek the higher range,
Could not betray the cul de sac, to folks just bent on change,
With no respect for mav'rick ways, or independent thought,
And not one frazzlin' idy, of the havoc bein' wrought,
By puttin' things on schedule, be it work, or man, or cow,
Till ways that make for bein' free, are bred plumb out, somehow.

So "Utah" turned and trotted off, to let them ol' hides be,
His heart a-beatin' lighter, just a-knowin' they were free.

J. B. Allen

WALLY BETTERIDGE

Prizewinning Packrat

Jack of all trades, master of most, this Montello collector braids good rawhide and shares the wealth.

Rather than use a keeper, some braiders prefer to loop the reins and romal together.

Montello, Nevada, is a town of ninety people "including cats and everybody out on the flats," as one resident remarks. It has six saloons, the kind of resident-to-bar ratio that was common at the turn of the century. Everybody in town meets in a saloon for coffee in the morning, when they pick up their mail from the tiny post office and gather to chat.

A few years back the Montello Lions Club voted Wally Betteridge "Citizen of the Year." The plaque he received is usually displayed in the Cowboy Bar unless Wally's got company coming, when he brings it home to show.

"I guess this means I can vote!" Wally laughs as he points to the plaque. He also has a bunch of plaques from Southern Pacific Railroad, many of them "Progress Through Safety Awards." He received one for "twenty consecutive years without reportable injury," one for "forty-one years of loyal, injury free service," and another for serving as "Grand Marshal of the first annual Montello Nevada Fourth of July parade, 1980."

Obviously, Wally is a man who's easy to like and knows the country. His family ranched in Grouse Creek, about twelve miles north of Montello. His grandfather pioneered there in the 1800s when it was known as Utah Territory. His father John continued the ranch, and it was from him that Wally learned about mecates and rawhide braiding. "My dad would make reins, hackamores, quirts. He just kept giving them to me, and I'd sell what he made for extra pocket money."

It was moonshine days, and Wally worked for $30 a month. He was a kid, and he had fun. "But the work always come ahead of the whiskey," he laughs. "Always does yet. You can't get to partying and then go to work, it don't work that way."

Wally grew up breaking horses. Once when he was showing off to a pretty neighbor girl, he jumped off his horse and twisted his knee. "We come down here to the doctor, and they didn't take pictures that long ago, they just used calipers to measure it. Dr. Belnap didn't lie to me. He said, 'I can't find a thing broke or out of place, but it's a complicated joint, and it'll probably always give you trouble.'" It always has. Wally was in his teens then and has been limping ever since. He did, however, manage to win the heart of the girl, Sally, and they married on February 17, 1923.

As Montello Parade Chairman, Wally got a fancy hat and a sheriff's badge.

When John Betteridge got tired of supplying his son with rawhide horse gear, he told Wally, "That's the last set of reins I'm going to give you. You are going to have to braid or buy them from now on."

Over more than sixty years working with rawhide, Wally has won plenty of prizes and ribbons for his braiding. He skins cows himself and tries to find ones without too many brands or abrasions. He uses Ivory or Castile bar soap to soften the hide and then cuts it with a pocketknife.

"I use a core sometimes, to make reins a little stronger, a little bigger. Sometimes I put two extra strings down the middle and braid over the top." Then, when they're damp, he rolls them on a board to make them smooth. He charges $80 a set, an absurdly low price considering the time needed to make them. "You can't make any money on it," he says. "I couldn't even board my family and work full time at it." It may take him two days to cut a hide up, and then he has to stretch it out on the fence. It takes him two more days to scrape off the hair. "If I could braid them as fast as I can get orders," he chuckles, "I could be a millionaire in a little while."

Sometimes he gets up at 5:30 in the morning and ties rawhide knots for reins. In the evening he may watch TV and tie some more. Each button takes about thirty minutes to make. "I like it. It keeps you out of the bar. It's a good pastime."

He doesn't think much of modern ropes. "If you got a half fast horse and go out and try to rope against the wind, you can catch yourself every time. But a rawhide rope is like a rock. It'll go against the wind—it's heavy." One of Wally's ropes was used for forty years. (Unfortunately, the man who owned it finally hung it on a wall and rats quickly made five pieces out of it.)

In the winter ropes get wet, but Wally says rawhide is stronger wet than dry, "and they get softer." However, to tie a horse to a post he'll choose a piece of cheap rope anytime. "Tie a horse up with rawhide and he'll break it, and there's $80 down the drain. This store-bought rope cost $2.50!"

Behind his house in Montello, Wally has brought in a number of sheds and filled them with plumbing and electrical supplies, carpentry tools and parts, all carefully arranged so that he can easily find them. The buildings are neatly set out on the dirt behind his house. Hides are soaking, getting ready for strings to be cut. He gives a lot away, fixes broken items, and offers them to

somebody with less than he's got. For the last few years the shops have been locked. "Used to be you didn't have to lock your doors around here," he says. "But it's changed since I was cowboying. The world is getting kinda bad."

Wally first worked as a cowboy but found that work on the railroad was more stable and lucrative. He worked for the Southern Pacific for forty-seven years, starting in March of '23. He was a blacksmith, an electrician's helper, a carpenter's helper, a plumber's helper. He worked at a rock-crushing plant, watching the machine in the control house. "That's all I had to do, just sit there, twelve hours a day. That's worse than working." When he asked for a bench and some tools, his boss asked what he was going to do.

"I told him, 'I don't give a damn. I'll make hammer handles or make nipples for the steam engine because they break every once in a while. I have got to have something to do.'"

Old iron spur with

brass rowel.

They gave him the tools, and he made spare parts for the railroad. At the same time he also started working on bits and spurs. "I could look out and see if everything was OK and then go on to work on the bench. It was a pastime. Of course, I couldn't take rawhide up there 'cause you can't work it when it gets dry."

For a while he worked in the water service, "anything to do with fuel, sewer, or water, based right here in Montello." He ran trips from Deeth to Lakeside at the edge of the Great Salt Lake, about one hundred and twenty miles. Whenever he was offered a promotion he turned it down.

"I had a chance to take promotions, but I would have had to leave home. You might be home one day a week, maybe two, or you won't get home for two or three weeks. I took less money and stayed home, and Sally and me, we just grew up together."

Sally and Wally had six children. Wally stayed home, a lot, and continued to prepare and work hides, making bosals, reins, hackamores, and quirts. He's always got several rawhide pieces in different stages of readiness. One needs grease, one needs a hondo. And there are always buttons to make.

U.S.-style bit, striped, with silver concho.

Sometimes the hides he gets aren't good. "See how fuzzy this is? Look at the difference. There's as much difference in hide as there is day and night. The fuzzy hides are coarse grained and you can cut them with a razor. This is not a good hide. You can tell what kind of hide you got the minute you start cutting it." Shoes are the same; some are good, some aren't. "They can't fool me in a leather shop anymore. I can go and bend the leather and tell them whether I want it or not."

Wally puts tallow fat on the rawhide, picks a hot day, and stretches it out, working it back and forth with his hand. Sometimes his hand gets so hot he thinks it's burning.

Neighboring ranchers call Wally when a cow dies. "I go and skin them. This black is where they lay down. It's blood and didn't come out of the hide. I made a rope out of that, and it looked like a rattlesnake hanging on the wall. It was speckled, a pretty rope. They give me a blue ribbon at the county fair on that, too."

He used to ride all day with the kids, but he quit riding when he was sixty-five. He has taught rawhiding to lots of young cowboys and jokes with everyone. "I'm getting old and cranky. Got up the right side of the bed this morning—you's lucky."

The railroad used to own Montello, but when the line was closed, the people in the area got together. "It was a lease deal, and they could move you off tomorrow, you know," Wally explains. "We bought the town, and the water here, so it belongs to us now." The railroad still owns plenty of ground in the area. Wally leases some railroad land for $5 a year, five years at a time.

When he retired, his bosses asked him to clear out the shops. They told him they wanted to be able to take everything out in a suitcase. So he took home plumbing fittings, acetylene torches, and electrical equipment—all with the railroad's blessing—and stored them in cubby holes in his sheds. "They come out here all the time and take what they need, anything they want. Sometimes they just bring something back to replace it. I imagine I could supply the entire town with anything it needs."

At first Wally and Sally had one lot in town, but they eventually acquired six. There are several small houses on the property. "I'd come home at night, peel out of my clothes, and have a bath. Then supper would be ready right away."

He and Sally enjoyed playing pool together in the local saloon and often won tournaments. Inside one of their houses there is a pool table. "We used to do a lot of pool playing, but you can't get people to get together anymore," Wally says slyly. "Might cost them $5, you know." For years, five teams played regularly. "But we took the money. We got trophies down there. She took the girls' one year, we took the doubles, and we had a lot of fun. It got to where they wouldn't let Sally and me play together." In fact, several plaques at the Cowboy Bar confirm Sally's and Wally's pool-playing skills.

Sally died a few years back after fifty-nine years of marriage. "I picked a good one," Wally sighs, "and I'm missing her now."

A couple of times a day he drives his orange Southern Pacific pickup across the tracks to feed his handful of cows and horses. Always, the animals recognize the truck and come bounding toward the corral. The horses, Honey and Rusty, are fat and lazy, treated with much affection by this aging cowboy even though he doesn't ride anymore.

Each morning he heads for the post office and then to Red's for a cup of coffee. "I have to go and harass people every day so they'll know I'm alive."

At Red's he orders a coffee royal. He says that's why he doesn't get sick, because there's whiskey in it. "I limit myself to two a day and that's it, so I never get the flu."

As he wanders back towards his house he turns back and waves. "Better stay a couple of days," he insists, "and get acquainted."

THE TINKER

There is one sort of cow hand that never is idle.
He is weavin' a cinch or he's fixin' a bridle;
He sits by the wagon or in the corral
And makes him a breast rig or braids a bosalle.

He has a grass rope and a rieta too,
With a quirt and hackamore nearly bran new.
He's got him a headstall that's made with a blind
And novelty spur rowells of different kinds.

He has got neckin' halters and spare hoggin' strings,
He has taps fer his stirrups and tossels and things.
A few extra jaw straps fer onder his bit;
A dehornin' saw and a shoein' outfit.

If he's in at the home ranch or out in the camps
He is workin' on hobbles and twitches and clamps.
Awls, needles, and waxends, and gauges, it's facts
The stuff he has gathered fills three gunny sacks.

He has new patent things to change stirrups perhaps,
And new patent fasteners fer latigo straps.
You boys have all seen him. He's one of the breed
That has got every thing a cow puncher don't need.

He never works hard but he has lots of friends.
He is willing to give, he is willing to lend.
He supplies the whole outfit, and the bosses have found
It's mighty convenient to have him around.

Bruce Kiskaddon

MARTIN BLACK Not Changing a Lick

Responsible for seven thousand bovines, this cowboy has become more than

handy with a horse, hair, hide, and rope.

This craftsman doesn't care for ropes with equal amounts of dark and light colors. He prefers designs with one main color and small areas in the contrasting shade.

He looks the part. And if buckaroos are supposed to be shy, he plays it to the hilt. He's as handsome as any cowboy on the silver screen but deplores photographers unless they focus on one of his well-trained horses at the Elko County Fair.

Martin Black is a buckaroo. He is also cow foreman for the Winecup Ranch in northeastern Elko County, Nevada. It is one of the largest ranches in the West, formerly owned by the mighty Utah Construction Company. Martin's background is ranching, his talent horses, but he also can braid rawhide and twist a pretty, fine-hair rope.

When he was growing up, there were few braiders or makers of fancy horse gear to pass the crafts along. "But anymore, just about everyone makes something. You can go to just about any ranch and find some really good braiders or hair-rope makers."

He was about six or seven when he started helping an old cowboy to make mecates. He says his first rope wasn't too bad, but in the past few years he's been making a dozen or more a year and they are looking mighty good. "I've only sold a few, but usually the cowboys here help me make 'em, and I'll give them one for helping me make another."

There are more than one hundred head of horses in the Winecup's cavvy, including eleven draft horses (the only ones that get their manes roached every year). Martin occasionally uses tail hair for practice, as when he made a six-strand rope. "Experimenting," he explains.

He can make bits, spurs, and chaps. He can braid leather and rawhide. But he prefers twisting hair. "I always wanted to make ropes. Once I got a machine, I didn't have any excuse not to make them." He has twisted ropes with master mecate maker Frankie Dougal of Jordan Valley, Oregon, but he doesn't think ropes with extra strands are worth the effort. "My first four-strand rope ain't too bad, but the six-strand I made is so crude I use it to tie up my bedroll."

Born in Bruneau, Idaho, not too far from Frankie and Chuck Dougal's place, Martin comes from a family of ranchers. As he buckarooed and worked, he slowly built a herd of his own. But times for beef weren't good, and he lost the entire herd.

Martin Black holds one braided and two twisted rawhide reatas. A twisted rope is faster to make but can't be spliced; if it breaks, the pieces will be used to tie up a bedroll.

"Those cows broke me," he says, "so I had to get my feet back on the ground financially by taking this job."

Martin has worked for the Winecup and the adjoining Gamble Ranch for several years. The Winecup's headquarters sits at five thousand feet in a broad, brush-covered valley. The outfit includes a couple of houses, a cook shack, tack rooms, bunkhouse, corrals, outbuildings, and sheds. Buckaroos seem to change with the seasons, constantly on the move. Martin understands because he's done it himself. He thinks it's good for cowboys to get experience at a variety of ranches before settling down.

Winters can be hard on the Winecup. The temperature often drops below zero. There can be up to eighteen inches of snow on the ground, and it can stay for months. Spring and fall can be muddy while summers are hot, dry, and dusty.

In summer the cattle—about seven thousand head—are turned out on the desert range, tended by eight buckaroos who start work long before the rooster announces dawn. The cowboys make sure that feed is good, that water is available, that fences are fixed, and the sick are doctored. In other seasons, they wean, sort, and ship. They feed livestock in winter, fix machinery and fence, assist calving heifers, and work with young horses. In spring they doctor and brand, then turn out on the desert again.

One cowboy specializes in starting colts, getting them "green broke" to add to the others' strings. Even though Martin Black would prefer that chore, he doesn't have time.

"I've got to supervise fence crews and irrigate, make sure the meadow hay is cut, and a lot of other things," he says. "The cowboys ride a lot and try to keep five to seven head of horses each, depending on how many colts they have in their string." He tries to start his own colts to replace older horses but doesn't get to ride as much as he'd like.

In high school Martin competed in rodeos, in cutting, team roping, calf roping, and bronc riding—"everything but bull riding and bareback." He would like to spend more time showing horses but dislikes the sport's politics. "It's a rich man's game and that's what I don't like about it. And there's no money in it."

*Close-up of rope
showing individual
strings that com-
prise a six-strand
mecate.*

An eight-string round braid worked into a ring like a turk's head: impossible to see the beginning or the end. Black saw one that had been made by Ernie Ladouceur in California and figured out how to make this curiosity. Other craftsmen say, "That's virtually impossible to make."

He has survived a lot of wrecks on the range and has the scars to prove it. One of his saddles has a spur track in the seat, made when he was falling off and the horse came down on top of him.

Each January, Martin and his wife Elaine get away from the ranch for a couple of days. They go to Elko to the Cowboy Poetry Gathering, where they see a lot of their friends. "That's one of the few times we get to go out," he says. They find someone to look after their energetic and noisy children, and Martin admits it's tough to get the same kidsitter twice.

It's rare for Martin Black to be seen in town, unless he's showing a horse at the Elko County Fair on Labor Day weekend. He uses his precious spare hours creating cowboy gear back at the ranch.

Although it's easy for him to get, this cowboy doesn't like using cow-tail hair for ropes. "It's a lot more work for less hair." Instead he prefers mane hair from the ranch's draft horses. "Draft horse mane is sometimes eighteen inches long, and the younger the horse, the softer the hair. It's just like a human's."

He uses a machine to pick the hair and sort it. Then he separates colors and rolls the hair into buns. He prefers to make ropes using two main colors with a dominant shade. He's partial to ropes with dots.

"I don't like mecates with stripes on them," he says. "I like to use three strings of one color, then another color to offset the other three."

He braids, too, making buttons, hackamores, and reins. He's twisted rawhide ropes and made braided reatas. "Twisting a rawhide rope is kind of a lazy man's way of making them. But with rawhide ropes you gotta be careful. They can break." He points to an old reata. "This rope here, I rolled a cow down a rimrock and it broke, got cut on the rocks."

For branding calves he likes the feel of a small rawhide rope because he doesn't have to use it hard. A smaller rope is easier to handle but, if you're using it every day, will break if you get too much weight on it. "But that big rope there," he says, "I couldn't break it. I tipped a cow plumb over backwards one time and she was going one way and I was going the other, and it never broke."

A heavy rawhide rope is more awkward to use, but Martin insists that they are stout. And he knows that if you dally badly, fingers that get caught between rope and saddle horn can be severed. "These ropes are kinkier, there's

Cowboys make gear
out of necessity. It
costs nothing but
time, and it's prac-
tical and beautiful.
Black is talented
enough to be able
to work with horse-
hair and rawhide,
and he likes to
trade. The barber-
pole rope is sorrel,
black, and white,
and was given to
Black by the noto-
rious rope maker
Blind Bob.

more twist goes through your hand and they can be dangerous to use. The advantage is they don't cost anything but time, if a hide is available."

He likes hides from skinny cows because he says they have more glue. "You can scrape the hair off and hold the hide up to a light and you can see through it. It's real glossy. With a fat cow's hide you can't do that. It doesn't have that glow. Another thing—a fat cow's rawhide is softer and not near as strong."

Martin likes to work on a hide soon after the cow is skinned so it doesn't rot. "Even if it's in a shed it's going to dry out," he says. Sometimes he'll freeze a hide, although he admits he has forgotten a few. "I drug one out that had been in the freezer over two years, but it was like I started it last week. I don't see anything wrong with freezing it, even though the next guy might tell you it isn't any good."

Over the years he's learned that craftsmen have their own quirky inclinations. When he was a kid starting to braid, one old cowboy told him never to use a black hide. Another told him that color doesn't make a difference. Martin was confused, but it turned out to be simple bovine bias. "A black cow ain't no good, so their hide ain't any good neither," the old cowboy had said. He raised Herefords and was prejudiced against Angus cattle. "One thing about this braiding," Martin says. "There are lots of opinions."

He rifles through a pile of horse gear. "First pair of spurs I made, a guy stole 'em," he says. "This is the second pair. Here's a headstall I made when I was in school, one of my first braiding attempts learning how to tie them knots. Them buttons take a long time, and there's a lot of room for error. If you don't have a trained eye, you wouldn't see them, unless it's really bad."

He works with leather but prefers rawhide for reins and ropes, even though it's harder to work. He says you can set down leather and come back to it, but you have to keep working the rawhide or it'll dry out. He has about twenty bits and headstalls in the tack room—most his creations—and says he needs them all.

"How many clothes have you got?" he asks rhetorically. "It's nice to have a variety of bridles for your horses because every horse isn't going to work the same way. When I put a horse in a bridle I might try three or four different ones on him. Whichever one he likes the best, that's the one I'll use."

Because he thought his silverwork was pretty primitive, he leaned toward braiding at first, with twisting hair as an afterthought. "But there was a lot of hair available on the ranch." His wife gets upset that he gives so much of his work away. "Elaine wants me to keep this stuff for my kids whether they turn out to be cowboys or not. I have been getting rid of it, giving it away, selling it as fast as I could make it."

Picking hair for ropes takes a lot of time. If a cowboy comes along and wants a rope, Martin asks him to help pick the hair and then helps him make one. Martin likes hair ropes because materials are cheaper than nylon. And he prefers the feel. He doesn't use nylon ropes on any horse gear. "All my stuff is hackamores with mecates on it."

Hair ropes aren't as strong as nylon ropes, but they're a whole lot prettier. And for hackamores, Martin prefers leather bosals to rawhide. "A lot of guys like rawhide hackamores, but I don't. That's why I buy tanned hides, cut the strings, and make everything myself." He says he's darned sure improved on the first few ropes he made, and believes when you reach a plateau that you have to start experimenting. He admires other creative buckaroos. "I admire people who accomplish something. I admire that in anybody."

Martin Black's dream is to have his own place, stocked with fat pregnant cows that are paid for. "I think that's pretty near everybody's goal," he smiles. "Cowboys like to have something of their own."

RAIN ON THE RANGE

When your boots are full of water and your hat brim's all a-drip,
And the rain makes little rivers dribblin' down your horse's hip,
When every step your pony takes, it purt near bogs him down,
It's then you git to thinkin' of them boys that work in town.
They're maybe sellin' ribbon, or they're maybe slingin' hash,
But they've got a roof above 'em when the thunder starts to crash.
They do their little doin's, be their wages low or high,
But let it rain till hell's a pond, they're always warm and dry.
Their beds are stuffed with feathers, or at worst with plenty straw,
While your ol' soggy soogans may go floatin' down the draw.
They've got no rope to fret about that kinks up when it's wet;
There ain't no puddle formin' in the saddle where they set.
There's womenfolks to cook 'em up the chuck they most admire
While you gnaw cold, hard biscuits 'cause the cook can't build a fire.

When you're ridin' on the cattle range and hit a rainy spell,
Your whiskers git plumb mossy, and you note a mildewed smell
On everything from leather to the makin's in your sack;
And you git the chilly quivers from the water down your back.
You couldn't pull your boots off if you hitched 'em to a mule;
You think about them ribbon clerks, and call yourself a fool
For ever punchin' cattle with a horse between your knees,
Instead of sellin' ribbons and a-takin' of your ease.
You sure do git to ponderin' about them jobs in town,
Where slickers ain't a-drippin' when the rain comes sluicin' down.
It's misery in your gizzard, and you sure do aim to quit,
And take most any sheltered job you figger you can git.
But when you've got your neck all bowed to quit without a doubt,
The rain just beats you to it, and the sun comes bustin' out!
Your wet clothes start to steamin', and most everywhere you pass
You notice how that week of rain has livened up the grass.
That's how it is with cowboys when a rainy spell is hit:
They hang on till it's over—then there ain't no need to quit!

S. Omar Barker

GLOSSARY

Explaining some common buckaroo terms.

BIT

> *Metal mouthpiece connected to reins, used to help control a horse.*
> *There are many types, used for different reasons, including half-*
> *breed, spade, snaffle, curb, and ring bits. There are also many styles,*
> *including Santa Barbara, cavalry, and lady's leg.*

BOSAL

> *A braided nosepiece, used with a mecate to train a horse. Goes over a*
> *horse's nose, but does not hold a bit.*

BUCKAROO

> *Corruption of the Spanish term* vaquero, *referring to cowboys from*
> *northern Nevada, SE Oregon, SW Idaho, and NE California.*
> *Buckaroos are some of the most flamboyant cowboys in dress*
> *and gear.*

BUCKING ROLLS

> *Leather swells attached to the front of a slick-fork saddle to help a*
> *cowboy stay in place when a horse gets to bucking.*

BUTTONS

> *The braided rawhide knots which help keep the sweat from rolling*
> *back along a set of reins. Also used for horsehair tassels and to tie off*
> *horsehair ropes.*

CANTLE

> *The upward-curving rear part of a saddle.*

CARVING

> *(also stamping, tooling) The art of making designs in relief on*
> *leather with a knife and beveling tools. Stamping also can refer to the*
> *use of pre-made stamps which indent the leather without cutting it,*
> *as in basket stamp.*

CAVVY

> *The group of horses used on a ranch.*

CHAPS

Pronounced "shaps," seatless pants made of leather, sometimes fur-covered, for protection from brush or cold, worn over regular pants.

CHINKS

Short chaps that reach just under the knees. Used in summer, and also for loading hay.

CHUTE WORK

To work off the range in the corrals, sorting, doctoring, weaning, and shipping cattle.

CINCH

A wide girth strap, usually cord but sometimes twisted horsehair, used to hold western saddles in place.

CONCHOS

(or conchas) Silver medallions, used to decorate horse gear.

DALLY

To wrap a rope around a saddle horn, to help hold the animal, after it is caught.

DOWELL

Used for hitched-hair work, the core of a piece, a base for pulling against.

FIADOR

(or Theadore) Small hair rope often tied around a horse's neck. Can thread through bottom of a small bosal, as a safety rope.

HACKAMORE

A bitless bridle of various designs used in breaking and training (from the Spanish word jáquima).

HEADSTALL

The straps which go over a horse's head and, together with bit and reins, form a bridle.

HITCHING

Artwork, usually made from horsehair, based on the half-hitch, including bridles, hat bands, belts, and quirts, using the tail hair of horses.

HOBBLES

A device used to keep horses from wandering when they are not tied up or confined in a corral or stall. Hobbles can be rope, rawhide, or leather and consist of two linked ankle bands which go around the horse's front feet.

HONDO

(or honda, or hondu) A ring of rope, rawhide, or metal on a lasso, through which the rope slides to make a loop.

JINGLEBOBS

Brass or steel additions to spur rowels, to make them ring.

LARIAT

Also known as lasso, from the Spanish "la reata," meaning rope.

LAST

A block or form shaped like a person's foot, on which shoes are made or repaired.

LEATHER

Processed, or tanned, hide.

MECATE

Spanish word for "hair rope," usually pronounced "McCardy," a combination rein and lead rope made of twisted horsehair. Also called mecarty or McCarty and used with a bosal to make a hackamore.

POPPER

The business end of a quirt or romal, usually two pieces of leather which can be used to tap the horse when necessary.

QUIRT

A short braided whip.

RAWHIDE

Unprocessed hide (processed hide is called leather).

REATA

(or riata) A rawhide rope, derived from the Spanish word reata, *meaning rope.*

RIDING POINT

The cowboys who ride ahead of the herd, to make sure they stay together. Riding flank *means staying at the side of the herd. Riding* drag *means following cattle, pushing the slowpokes from the back.*

RIGGING

Metal rings which hold cinch straps on a saddle.

RODEER

A gathering of cowboys, usually assembled to separate stock on the range during fall roundup.

ROLLER

Wheel in mouthpiece of bit, often copper, used to entertain a horse.

ROMAL

A quirt attached to a set of reins.

ROUGH-OUT

The inside, or rough side, of a piece of tanned hide. The outside of a hide is smooth.

ROWELS

The circular parts that spin on the back of spurs.

SKIVING

The process of shaving off bits of rawhide or leather until strings are all the same thickness and boot and saddle joints are smooth. If strings are not skived before rawhide braiding, the final product will not be even.

SLICK FORK

A type of saddle which does not have swells on either side of the horn, favored by buckaroos.

SOOGAN

(or sougan) A quilt or comforter in a cowboy's bedroll.

STAMPEDE STRING

A string of rawhide, hitched hair, or leather that goes under the chin to keep a cowboy hat secure, safe from the wind. While a cowboy is seriously chasing cattle, the last thing he needs is to lose his hat.

SWELLS

(or pommels) Bulges on either side of the saddle horn. They come in a variety of sizes, from nonexistent (slick fork) to very large.

TAPADEROS

Leather-covered stirrups which enclose the front of a cowboy's boot to protect it. From the Spanish tapaderas, *meaning covers.*

TEEPEE

Small canvas tent used by cowboys out on the range. (These tents are not like Indian tipis.)

TREE

The wooden frame of a saddle.

TURK'S HEAD

(or turk) A turban-like knot made on the end of a mecate.

WILDRAG

Large cowboy scarf, used for warmth in bad weather, and to protect the nose and throat from dust.

WRANGLE

To herd livestock, especially saddle horses.

CREDITS

"Noon Break" by Gwen Petersen and Jeane Rhodes is from *Tall in the Sidesaddle: Ranch Woman Rhymes* (Big Timber, Montana: P/R Press, 1986). Copyright 1986 P/R Press. Used by permission of Gwen Petersen.

"You Can't Fool a Kid" by Carl "Skinny" Rowland is from *Truths, Lies & Otherwise* (Helena, Montana: Carl Rowland, 1987). Copyright 1987 Carl Art Rowland. Used by permission of the author.

"Hats, Britches, Boots, Spurs 'n Chaps" by Gwen Petersen and Jeane Rhodes is from *Cowpunchers, Sheep Herders, and Plain Pig Farmers: Wild West Limericks* (Billings, Montana: Falcon Press Publishing Co., 1985). Copyright 1985 Gwen A. Petersen and Jeane F. Rhodes. Used by permission of Gwen Petersen.

"Kindred Spirits" by J. B. Allen is from *Water Gap Wisdom* (Whiteface, Texas: J. B. Allen, 1990). Copyright 1990 J. B. Allen. Used by permission of the author.

Most of the photographs in this book were taken by the author and are copyrighted by her. Photos taken by others are listed below.

The photographs on pages 51 and 55 are by D. W. Frommer. Copyright 1993 D. W. Frommer. Used by permission of the photographer.

The photograph on page 96 is by Jim Le Goy of the Le Goy Studio, Reno, Nevada. Copyright 1993 Jim Le Goy. Used by permission of the photographer.

The photographs on pages 102 and 103 are by Roche Bush of the Fox Foto Shop, Elko, Nevada. Copyright 1993 Roche Bush. Used by permission of the photographer.

Captions for front and back matter photographs:

page i: Paul swings his catch rope, practicing, while the other buckaroos work a colt, shoe a horse, or relax for a while before the wagon cook has supper ready.

pages ii–iii: Buckaroo spurs, made by Jeremiah Watt.

page v: Jon Griggs entertains Grant, the young son of the cow boss, Doug Groves.

page vi: Elko County buckaroos Jon, Mike, Nathan, and Nick start to push cows out from winter pasture to spring range on the desert.

page x: Horsehair mecates, made by William Stuart.

page xiii: Intricate, hand-dyed hitched-hair quirt, made by Alfredo Campos.

page 1: Nathan holds the herd.

page 3: Hand-engraved belt buckle, made by Al Pecetti.

page 190: Rawhide throatlatch with horsehair tassels, made by Jeff Minor.

page 196: Hitched-hair and leather cuffs by Doug Krause.